HOW *JAMES BOND* SAVED MY LIFE

DAVID HARKIN

The Book Guild Ltd

First published in Great Britain in 2024 by
The Book Guild Ltd
Unit E2 Airfield Business Park,
Harrison Road, Market Harborough,
Leicestershire. LE16 7UL
Tel: 0116 2792299
www.bookguild.co.uk
Email: info@bookguild.co.uk
X: @bookguild

Copyright © 2024 David Harkin

The right of David Harkin to be identified as the author of this
work has been asserted by them in accordance with the
Copyright, Design and Patents Act 1988.

All rights reserved. No part of this publication may be
reproduced, transmitted, or stored in a retrieval system, in any form or by any means,
without permission in writing from the publisher, nor be otherwise circulated in
any form of binding or cover other than that in which it is published and without
a similar condition being imposed on the subsequent purchaser.

Typeset in 11pt Minion Pro

Printed and bound by CPI Group (UK) Ltd, Croydon, CR0 4YY

ISBN 978 1916668 409

British Library Cataloguing in Publication Data.
A catalogue record for this book is available from the British Library.

*I dedicate this book to my beautiful wife, Golda,
my dearest son, David, and any young person seeking
distraction, hope and inspiration.*

Author's Note

Just a word of caution. If viewing any film title mentioned in this book. It is advisable to check the BBFC (British Board of Film Classification) rating of each individual film, as every individual person is different, and themes and content may not be suitable.

Acknowledgement

I want to express my gratitude to my grandmother, Annie Harkin, for introducing me to the world of cinema many years ago.

I will always cherish the time we shared together.

The title *How James Bond Saved My Life* refers to a conversation with a mental health consultant who said that during my formative years as a non-verbal child, "James Bond had saved my life," suggesting that the fictional character of James Bond was the underlying role model in the early part of my life.

How James Bond Saved My Life explores why a fictional character dreamed up by Ian Fleming over a half-century ago saved my life. I detail my family and school life, growing up, struggling at school, searching for cinematic role models, while considering the importance of cinema therapy and cinematic role models regarding young people.

Through this viewpoint is a potted history of cinema through the eyes of someone who grew up requiring speech therapy and additional help throughout his troubled school days. Watching escapist cinema, like James Bond movies, is a form of "cinema therapy". The practice of watching films and getting lost in the world of *Black Panther* or *Ready Player One*, immersing yourself in the colour of *Fantasia* or the comedy of the Marx Brothers, is like having an ice cream on a scorching hot day – it's an escape from life, a relief.

As a media facilitator and qualified youth worker, I work with young people on media and film projects.

During these sessions with young people, I discuss and, more importantly, listen to young people and their varying opinions on cinematic role models, inspiring characters, and escapist entertainment.

Certain cinematic role models, like Auggie in *Wonder* can connect people to characters and situations. Inspiring stories of courage, like fighting Nazis in *The Heroes of Telemark*, or being true to yourself, as the brave Alike in *Pariah*, can help build resilience and independence.

When a young person can't find a positive role model at home, school or at a youth club, they may look elsewhere. I know I did; I looked at the silver screen.

Like Cecilia (Mia Farrow) in Woody Allen's *The Purple Rose of Cairo*, who watches the same film repeatedly to escape reality, cinema offers us a respite from life – a fantasy world where we can break free from our anxieties.

Focusing its lens entirely on cinematic role models plucked from films rather than television or gaming, *How James Bond Saved My Life* hopes to expand the conversation on the importance of cinematic role models and their impression and influence on young people.

So, why listen to me? My background is in film studies, gaining a master's degree in the subject, writing about cinema, and winning a few film awards along the way. I professionally engage with young people on film and media programmes with the Education Authority in Northern Ireland and, in the past, have worked with many other individuals on film-related programmes with Northern Ireland Screen and The National Lottery.

Growing up, struggling at school, struggling to speak "properly", the onscreen antics of James Bond skiing down mountains, skipping over crocodiles and hanging on to helicopters resonated with an impressionable young boy with special educational needs (SEN). Bond was a distraction, undoubtedly a larger-than-life role model that would transcend the confines of my fourteen-inch television and allow a five-year-old boy an escape into a world of spy rings, suave sophistication and elegant charm.

How James Bond Saved My Life revisits my cinematic education growing up as I searched for role models who could build my confidence and help me find an identity and a connection to a broader world. As a young child undergoing speech therapy, it took me years to feel confident enough to string sentences together. So, I needed to find larger-than-life role models – fearless role models who I could connect with and empower me.

I hope you find this journey through cinema beneficial as I recall and reflect on the films and role models that inspired and ultimately changed my life and, hopefully, the lives of many young people.

David Harkin, September 2023

Part One

How did I know I needed cinematic role models?

Fade in: a working-class area of Derry, Northern Ireland. What was the initial loss of confidence that required me to search for fictional characters? Well, it was a typical school day, which got ugly. This was the catalyst of why I stared at our rented television in the corner of our living room, searching for a life outside of my own – searching for cinematic role models.

(Cue a suitable voice-over artist) I was five years old, and as I say, it was a typical school day; I had just left a nearby shop, procuring my Club biscuit for break time. The street was busy, with parents standing next to traffic lights, children stepping off school buses and everyone in their private little worlds. I dreamed of that Club biscuit, the crunch, and the taste of sugary orange with milky chocolate. Suddenly this idyllic thought pattern morphed into "WTF territory" when a car door swung open on the edge of the street. The car was bright red, and the sun's rays

bounced off the bonnet, revealing dust and dirt. Inside the car was a man with tight curly hair and a friendly smile.

You can see where this is going – this may be a trigger warning for some, so, you may wish to skip on to the next bit. He beckoned me closer, encouraging me. There was nothing familiar about him. I felt numb. I felt time slowing down. Suddenly I began to feel a shooting pain running through my body. My small hands were sweaty, and my heart was pounding. It was paralysing. It was the first time I had felt fear. The fear that a five-year-old child should never experience.

There was a smell of stale cigarettes and red leather as the man held out a small white paper bag filled with sweets. The bag was crumpled as if it had been squashed in his pocket all day. I climbed onto the shiny red leather of his passenger seat and reached over to pick a favourite toffee from his bag of sweets. But before anything else could happen, my younger brother Barry pulled me down from his passenger seat and back safely into the street.

I never saw the man again, and he's as much a stranger to me now as he was in 1984. That day, all those years ago, I didn't say anything. I didn't call out. I just couldn't. I was only beginning to speak; I had been non-verbal for five years. As a non-verbal child, I had little confidence, and I jumped into that car with little thought of the consequences.

There was another incident at a sports centre, near a running track, where a man exposed himself. I was skipping school, or "dobbing" school as we called it. I sat on a bench, pretending to watch runners running around in a circle. When a man sat next to me, took out his genitals and began rubbing them, I was too naive to even think that there was anything sexual going on, but I found it disturbing.

The man looked at me, his hands massaging his balls (bet you wish you had skipped this part, eh?), his eyes widening. I stared back and soon left him and his balls on the sports track. I returned to the sports centre foyer and got lost in a copy of *The Beano*.

These incidents were fleeting, but they obviously affected me. They pushed me towards a need for cinematic role models – a world where life didn't feel like deleted scenes from *Last House on the Left*.

For My Eyes Only

This part could be my prequel, my backstory, explaining why I or anyone else would need cinematic role models. These parts are also the boring parts of biographies which I usually skip. With that in mind, I only promise to include my early life's "WTF moments" – the areas of life that required cinema therapy, i.e. onscreen characters to relate to or a film to unwind and relax with.

Now, if you're reading this next bit and thinking, I was the class prefect and school ambassador, and school life was great; I met my future husband at school – what's this guy talking about? The need for cinematic screen heroes is not exclusive to me or school bullying.

Everyone needs a break from life at some point. I can remember one of the special features on a *Star Trek* DVD. Captain Kirk, or the bald guy from *X-Men*, was talking about police officers in America. How, after a long day "on the beat", arresting drug dealers and rescuing children from abusive parents, this particular policeman would stick on *Star Trek* to escape their reality – and in the case of Captain Kirk, to literally see another world.

This backward glance at my school days was my reason to escape reality and find James Bond; maybe yours is to get away from another one of life's challenges, a loss of confidence or the loss of a boyfriend – whatever it is, everyone needs a space to switch off and tune into another world.

Blind Eye

Just after starting school, when I began speech therapy. I remember both parents, my dad Michael and mother Grainne-Maeve, taking me from school, removing me from class and bringing me to the health centre to undergo weekly speech therapy.

This "health" centre stunk of cigarettes and yesterday's beer. But I remember hearing hushed voices whispering about my "condition" as if I couldn't hear them.

In a small room at the back of the building, a doctor suggested I was deaf and couldn't hear anything. I stood by a window staring out, presumably at the car park, probably wondering what was for lunch.

My dad was also in the room and vehemently disagreed that I was deaf. To prove I was deaf, a doctor rang a small bell and convinced himself that I was indeed deaf because I didn't turn around to face him. Like a yarn you could dine out on for a decade, my dad said my name to prove the doctor wrong. I was still staring out the window when I heard my name; I swung my head from the window and looked at my dad and the doctor on the other side of the room. I ignored the bell and the doctor but not my name. I wasn't deaf; I was non-verbal.

David is Forever

I was born Damien. Damien was the one who didn't talk. Zero to five years old, it was all Damien. He was the one that didn't speak a word. So, when I began to talk and slowly get my sentences in the correct order, one of the first things I did was change my first name.

Years later, the same consultant who suggested that "James Bond had saved my life" further indicated that Damien was my "Clark Kent" and David became my "Superman". That drawing inspiration from onscreen role models became my superpower.

So, I changed my first name from Damien to David at a young age. Perhaps I felt that the pressure of not talking at such an early age could be hidden by removing or hiding a name associated with it. Maybe in my subconscious, there was a feeling of being a lesser person, a strong sense that I couldn't do things and that I couldn't cope. It felt fed into me from an early age.

However, little did I know that this was just the preamble of dealing with school life as a child with special educational needs. It became clear that primary school was merely the calm before the storm.

Yesterday Never Lies

I always like any part of a book that begins with a quote from a better author, so I won't sway from the cliché.

The British novelist L. P. Hartley, in *The Go-Between*, wrote that "the past is a foreign country: they do things differently there." In the 1980s and '90s, it did feel that the education system placed the burden of learning solely on the pupil. As I had trouble communicating, I had to repeat my first year at school: same books, same teacher, different pupils.

There was a different educational culture back then. Teachers would slap a child's hand with rulers wrapped in elastic bands, and children were seen and not heard. You don't need to watch a frame of *The Breakfast Club* to see that the 1980s is the distant past, and many things were different then – the sound of chalk on a blackboard, the blur of the overhead projector, and shell suits. Too many people wore those shiny shell suits. Boy, they were shit.

What was depressing about the 1980s, apart from the lack of fashion sense, was the lack of pastoral care for a boy who was non-verbal. It left me feeling stupid, a feeling that lasted all of my childhood at school.

As some of you will remember from an edgy episode of *Grange Hill*, I remember at school, there being two types of children – "slow" and "normal". I didn't make these rules and never questioned them; hey, what did I know? I was a child being told I was "slow". I knew I fell into the "slow" group with the stares and hushed conversations. I wasn't alone. Later at secondary school, I found many others clumped together as the "slow ones". I was also aware that bullying or bullies didn't discriminate. Most people at school were bullied; it was just easier to mock the more vulnerable children.

The world was different, and society's attitudes to

mental health, gender politics, and disability were very different than they are today. People were more stupid. Didn't you read that bit about shell suits?

It's refreshing today regarding my son, David, who also has special educational needs, or in my workplace when I'm working with young people, that the approach is entirely different. Terms and meanings such as SEND (special educational needs and disabilities) or ADHD (attention deficit hyperactivity disorder) are now becoming a part of the vernacular as parents wait outside the school gates.

However, some people haven't learned anything from the past; some still think Bros were a good pop group and some push the stigma and culture of being "different" to new levels of depravity with school bullying. When I was at school, being "slow" was the crude expression slapped on you regardless of whether you were autistic, suffering from hearing loss, dyslexic or, in my case, overcoming speech and language challenges. These were the days when there were only four terrestrial television channels, Sony Walkmans and scrunchies – no scripted reality programmes, Netflix or "documentaries" on Botoxed celebrities.

At school, there was an attitude people believed that "Oh, he can't speak properly; therefore, he must be stupid". Thankfully today it is getting better. In terms of pastoral support, young people have a clearer view of where the goalposts are. With support and a better understanding of inclusion, if you are a young individual with special educational needs, school life has significantly improved since the 1980s and '90s.

If you imagine a school with interior design from the

'70s and the integrity of a sewer rat, that might give you an impression of my secondary school, St Peter's. When I first found this out, it was a crushing disappointment as the school was in the same area that some of my family lived in.

These years were rife with bullying. Still getting to grips with language, I needed more confidence in speaking. Simple mispronunciations would be remembered, magnified and spread like propaganda throughout the class. I didn't have a chance in a male-only school filled with five hundred boys, with heads full of Page 3 girls and stories of the then-current Troubles in the north of Ireland.

This was Northern Ireland in the early 1990s. Everyone claimed their dad was in the I.R.A.; maybe they were, I didn't care, but it brought a bravado and a swagger that most classmates brought with them every day. Ironically, when I did string a sentence together, teachers would hear me but never listen to me. It was, in a word, depressing.

Live Another Day

The main building of my secondary school was all brown bricks and dirty wooden doors decorated with dirty shoe marks and poorly misspelt graffiti. Most of the teachers would be stuffing their faces with cream buns, as the students stared out the window at a nearby farm; a farmer, maybe middle-aged, shuffling rubbish into a skip.

One time at St Peter's, to try and help curb the bullying, one of the teachers had an idea, probably formulated in the staff room over tea and custard creams, to pair me with a "bodyguard". Like a scene from *Drillbit*

Taylor, this bodyguard and would-be saviour was one of the boys who bullied me. As he entered the room with a grin sharp enough to open a tin of beans, I knew the daily gauntlet of getting the bus home would be particularly challenging later that afternoon. But this was nothing. The level of bullying was frequent and was also – and I use this word carefully – traumatic. It was a traumatic experience.

St Peter's was like a twisted version of *Waterloo Road*. Snot would hang like party streamers from the ceiling while also taking up residence on the bannisters. Drawing pins would rest on vacant chairs for the next occupant to sit on. Excrement would decorate the bog walls in a toilet area, as you were held down and spat on.

During one term, I got to know a tag team of bullies quite well between the dinnertime break and the first afternoon class. There was a short grassy hill next to the football pitch; one of the bullies made me run up the hill, only for the other one to kick me back down it. How long this continued, I don't know. I've probably blanked most of it out. Each day was a living nightmare.

A legacy of the Christian Brothers, a school my dad had attended, my new secondary school was a terrible place. Before being dumped at secondary school, I had heard of the school while still at primary school. It sounded like something out of *The Bash Street Kids*, the worst stories regarding pea shooters and pupils being forced to eat bus tickets. The reality was far worse. This place was a school for bullies. It would have topped the national list if "learning to be a bully" could have been GCSE graded.

As I look over this text, searching for spelling mistakes, it sounds like I had gone to school in the backstreets of Dickensian London. But I hated every second of it. There was no hiding place for children like me who had difficulty communicating.

A View to the Past

Now in his forties, Tommy, who I met as an adult and who would become a life-long friend, also attended St Peter's, but I never knew him at school; like me, he had difficulty communicating, and just like me, Tommy was also mercilessly bullied. Tommy told me how his heart would sink as he spotted the school bus shifting its gears as it made its way towards him.

The sight of St Peter's brown, oppressive "prison-like" walls sent a shiver down Tommy's spine. Due to a severe lack of confidence at school, Tommy needed help and more support, so, like me, he would spend much of his days finding ways to dodge school.

Whereas I would ultimately find refuge and strength in the world of James Bond, Tommy found salvation in Rocky and Rambo. Sneaking into cinema screenings of *Rambo: First Blood Part II* was Tommy's departure from the real world – his private escape. He would leave school at fifteen, never looking back, yet never forgiving his tormentors. Bullying is not exclusive to me or, indeed, Tommy. Many have survived its trauma.

For me, I just needed a break from life – a place to park the bullshit. St Peter's never offered me any confidence or peace. Like the opening scene in Brian De Palma's *Carrie*, where the central character experiences menstruation for the first time in a school shower room, I only found out about sperm when it was rubbed on my face and lips at school. It was disgusting.

Having skipped primary seven and never having a chance to have a go at the transfer test, I had no choice in choosing my secondary school. So, it resulted in being shipped to that hellhole of a secondary school. Every day, bullying was never far away. It could be slamming your head off a bus window, pushing you down a flight of stairs or spitting on your lunch.

Once, I spotted a strange car outside my house; it was from social services. They were enquiring about me skipping so many school days (ninety-two in my first year) and threatened me with a possible move to St Pat's, a hangover of the old borstal system – a prison for kids. I remember telling the social worker I didn't "give a fuck" about going to St Pat's. Hardly the vocabulary of the smooth-talking James Bond, but it seemed as if everyone had forgotten that running away from a problem doesn't make it go away.

One of my last encounters with a teacher at the school was when I was told not to bother to do any GCSEs, my final year exams, as it would be a waste of money for the school. It's no wonder my mental health was deteriorating.

Digging up the past, it seems that the only thing I learned at secondary school was how to swerve it. My school even played the film *Ferris Bueller's Day Off* as an end-of-term treat for the class. A comedy where the main character pretends to be sick so he can dodge school and enjoy a day with his girlfriend and his best friend. On reflection, viewing this cult '80s classic in a school classroom only normalised my habit of doing the same – minus the cute girlfriend.

You Only Live Once

One incident occurred that, in retrospect, brought the whole notion of cinematic role models full circle. Two years after leaving school, I was with my grandmother on my mother's side. There had been a death in the family – after a short illness, my granda Sproule died. He had enjoyed telling tales of footballers in long baggy shorts and bare-knuckle fistfights at the back of a fish shop, but now he was gone.

So, to keep my granny Sproule company, my brother Barry and one of my best friends Marty, stayed at my grandmother's house. My granny was asleep, and after several cups of tea in another room at the top of her large house, Barry, Marty and I remarked how utterly bored we were.

So, with nothing to do, I spotted a few dusty paperback books. My eyes panned across the bookshelf, and I spotted a series of what looked like diaries written by my granny. I could have listened to the radio or waited eight years for YouTube to be invented, but as there was no TV and the conversation between Barry, Marty and I had dried up, I lifted one of the diaries and began reading. I spotted one of the diaries from my birth year.

It was all about the milkman and the price of eggs – it was boring. But I kept reading the diaries for reasons I still don't know. I flicked through the pages, searching for my birthday. I found the diary entry for it, but there was no mention of me. My brother Barry who had witnessed my investigation into the diaries, looked at me, his face frozen. I asked him, "Why is there no mention of me?"

I read through the diary, searching for a comment or, if lucky, a full diary entry that would mention more about me. Nothing in the diary said anything about me.

As I entered the month of July, I found a comment concerning a child from a children's home. I looked across the room, and pointing the question at no one in particular, I said, "Am I adopted?" The answer was yes. It was a family secret that everyone besides me knew about.

I was born in a different place with another name. As a week-old baby, I was abandoned and given up to the authorities to find a new home. I had lived with nuns at a mother-and-baby home before being shipped to a foster home. Subsequently, I discovered I was a child of the Northern Ireland Troubles, with a biological Catholic mother and a biological Protestant father in the UDR (Ulster Defence Regiment).

Growing up in a nationalist area of Derry, I was aware of the Ulster Defence Regiment's links to paramilitary organisations and their brutality towards Catholics, so I was pleased to discover my biological (and jailbird) father, before I was born, wanted little to do with me. Besides, I knew who my dad was; he was the guy that took me to speech therapy when I was five years old.

Keeping my granny Sproule company that night changed my life. Not long after reading those diaries, I began to mentally join the dots in my head, my brain suggesting that the trauma involved in my adoption may have resulted in my future communication challenges.

The revelation that I was adopted also made me consider my search for an identity in a male cinematic role model, as searching for an escape, a way out. Much later, when discussing this with a mental health consultant, she pointed me to a newspaper article in *The Guardian* by Vanessa Thorpe entitled "'Me against the world': why superheroes are so often orphans".

It detailed how a museum in England celebrated and recognised the connection between fictional heroes like Spider-Man, Batman and Superman and their relationship with adoptees.

There were parallels to be found between cinematic heroes and adoptees, both groups who need to build an identity and who both feel like outsiders. The abandonment issues, the search for resilience, the search for an identity and the search for a larger-than-life role model all resonated with me. It's no wonder that I had been searching for these larger-than-life characters since the early 1980s.

It was inevitable that James Bond would affect me so much. Within fandom, some films or characters resonate with you more. Some characters are a conductor of a more profound feeling within your personality. Simply put, Bond had filled a gap and fixed a hole.

When I was a child in the 1980s, Bond had an extensive catalogue of films numbering a dozen, all on television, and unlike *Superman* and *Star Wars* films, not glued solely to the Christmas and Easter television schedules.

Like Superman and Batman, Bond was a loner, but with a foster mum and dad in M and a grandfather in Q. After reading that diary, I knew why I had searched for cinematic role models, for an escape from trauma.

The Family Who Loved Me

Everyone has a family; the guys at work have a family, your friends have a family. Hitler had a family – okay, they might not have loved him, but he had a family. We can agree people have families. These people typically become our role models in early life. But I needed more than garden-variety role models. As a young non-verbal child, I needed larger-than-life role models. I needed cinematic role models. Yet, in the interest of social context, social environment and word count. Let's take a look back at my family.

I was surrounded by three brothers and a single television, and for a while, it was a fourteen-inch television, small and white – rented from Radio Rentals. Unlike today's over-saturated world of streaming services, where every film is a touch of a button away, thirty years ago, recording a film or anything else off the television would require careful planning.

It would mean setting up the timer on your video recorder or staying up half the night to record your favourite film. If you didn't have a blank VHS cassette, you would stick a piece of sticky tape in the corner of an existing cassette, allowing the cassette to be "taped over".

There were only four channels, maybe a few more if you stuck a coat hanger in the back of the TV. Maybe with some jiggery-pokery, you could tune in two channels from the Republic of Ireland. Both would show films, usually uncut, and it was a chance to see movies with fewer advertisement breaks. If something was on television, you had to watch it or record it; there was no catch-up service.

Although we four brothers shared the same cheap deodorant as teenagers, our opinions of films differed significantly; Christy, my eldest brother, watched Bela Lugosi and Klaus Kinski films, typically at 3 am on the weekends. Demonstrated by the length of hair he grew; Christy went through various phases of rebellion. Long when a goth, short when an anarchist and bald when a skinhead. Although I never took any of that seriously, I considered him a "college boy" as he attended St Columb's College, which was more upmarket than my school.

Two years younger than Christy was Robin; Robin was the most intellectual of us, an avid reader and artist. Robin probably invented the word "binge-watching". He would watch Jackie Chan films on a loop. No TV-am or BBC Breakfast for me – I ate my cornflakes in the morning with *Armour of God* playing in the background.

I saw Barry, my younger brother, at primary school every day. As I was kept back a year at school due to communication challenges, I entered Barry's class when I repeated primary one. Barry helped me with basic sign language and facial gestures. Armed with a high IQ, Barry loved Jerry Lewis films and hated *Match of the Day*. Only the one year separating us, as a teenager, he was able to build a computer from bits of motherboards and scraps of wire – a regular *MacGyver*.

Growing up within that social environment, with my dad, Michael, a keen film enthusiast and first-generation Bond fan, to the mix, my influences came from different directions. Yet, I grew close to my granny Harkin due to circumstances beyond my control. She played a significant role in my early life for many reasons, one being that my dad lived with her for most of my childhood due to the break-up of my parents' marriage when I was still in primary school. The other important reason is that she loved films and Hollywood cinema.

From Granny with Love

Growing up in the 1980s and '90s, we rarely went to the cinema or "the Pictures" as we called it. Throughout the Troubles in Northern Ireland, the cinema wasn't always the safest place to spend a few hours.

I can remember that during the release of a Bond film, the cinema was evacuated due to a bomb scare. So, like a flock of sheep, we stood outside the cinema, waiting – a collective bunch of nitwits staring at each other as if we could read each other's minds. It seems strange now, but to everyone I knew, during the tail end of the Troubles, the culture of ongoing bomb scares, and the fact that people had become so used to bomb scares, almost left the impression that a bomb scare was more of an inconvenience than a threat of impending death.

On another occasion, during the release of one of the *Star Trek* films, the upstairs part of the cinema was all splintered glass and shattered masonry from a recent bomb blast. Yet again, we all stood outside the cinema, waiting to go back in to see the rest of the film, perhaps just wishing to exchange the outside world of the Troubles for the cosy world of the Klingons. It was a strange and scary time growing up.

So, coupled with the break-up of my parents' marriage and the madness of the Troubles, my granny

Harkin's house was a safe haven. Picture the scene, no Netflix, no Disney+ – you decided what you wanted to watch without the help of a faceless algorithm. Okay, there were downsides to a world without the internet – you had to speak to a human when ordering food – but you see my point.

Barry and I would spend most weekends at my granny Harkin's house, and she would develop into a live-action precursor to a DVD commentary, filling my head with stories of the 1930s and '40s movie stars. Her eyes were bright as she spoke fondly of seeing *The Invisible Man* and *Samson and Delilah*, some of which would be shown regularly on television.

Yet, on a Saturday morning, the television was never on. My granny would be at the shops buying, among many other things, apple turnovers and gorgeous cream fingers. My granny knew that my wee brother and I would leave lights on and generally waste what she called "the electric light bill". She was a great woman, but she had grown up in another era, so things like the television would only be switched on when required.

My granny had a twenty-one-inch television, no flat screens back then, with sound bars and 4K resolution. Unlike today where sixty-inch flat screens are pinned in pride of place above the fireplace, in those days the television looked like a bit of furniture, sitting in the corner, with a large bowl of fruit and an ashtray on top of it. Still, the picture quality was excellent for the time, but then I knew no better, and watching television was a shared viewing experience. Unlike today where everyone is watching on different devices and in other rooms, back then, in the '80s and '90s, we all watched *Eastenders* and *The Great Escape* together within the same four walls.

Best to imagine Morgan Freeman narrating this section perhaps. Born at the beginning of the twentieth century, my granny Harkin, had grown up with cinema as it had developed and changed from a nineteenth-century novelty with magic lantern shows to a worldwide industry. How cool it would have been to be alive during the early twentieth century when the genesis of motion pictures as an art form and a platform for mass entertainment was gathering pace.

My granny always loved those classic films from the Hollywood studio system, where every studio had its stable of designers, special effects departments, directors and stars. She loved those movies from the 1950s like *The Ten Commandments* and *Ben Hur*.

When the biblical borefest *The Robe*, starring Richard Burton, was released in a new process called CinemaScope. My granny told me that the Palace Cinema in Derry was the first cinema in our city to screen *The Robe* in CinemaScope and stereophonic sound and how it "shook the walls of the cinema". During the 1950s when a television set was a tiny box in your living room, these unique cinema experiences allowed my granny and many others a new sensory experience on an epic scale, something a little black and white television set could never compete with.

With my dad earning a few bucks playing in bands, late on a Friday night, after the usual run of Channel 4 and BBC sitcoms, there would be a Universal horror film or a Roger Corman film, which kicked my granny's memory into gear. There would be a yarn, a story or a one-sided discussion on a forgotten movie star or long-lost film, a thread of a memory kept alive in her heart.

Unfortunately, older people are generally seen as an invisible demographic. Yet, in terms of my relationship with my grandmother, older people can be a portal to the past. They have a lifelong stream of knowledge and experience worth tapping into, the mistakes and successes in life, and the journey they were on before they even met you.

My granny was no expert, but she enjoyed speaking to me about all these curious and interesting titbits of information she had read or heard about – tall tales about going to the cinema and falling in love with film stars such as Johnny Weissmuller and Victor Mature. Conversations with my granny would spin from her friends and neighbours fighting the First World War to her discussions on early silent cinema whose turn it was to make a cup of tea.

In the 1930s and '40s, when early twentieth-century cinema was getting revisited, my granny would go to the local cinema to watch masterpieces from the silent era. Sitting in a cinema in the 1940s, watching ambitious silent films from the 1910s, such as *The Birth of a Nation* and *Intolerance*, must have looked prehistoric to my grandmother, who in the 1940s was watching the colourful beauty of *Black Narcissus* and *Meet Me in St. Louis*.

Today, writing this, it feels like my granny was a million years old, as she was alive to witness D. W. Griffith developing narrative structure and Cecil B. DeMille establishing spectacle and grandeur during the silent era of cinema. My grandmother and her contemporaries had watched cinema grow and blossom into an art form and film industry.

I found many things about my granny Harkin fascinating; she was resilient, strong and kind, and I appreciated her memory of early cinema. Having lived through two World Wars, my granny was like a jukebox of relatable stories, some tragic, some funny. She would tell tales of going to the cinema sixty years earlier, how she had watched Laurel and Hardy films in the 1930s and how she had laughed at Charlie Chaplin in *The Gold Rush* in 1925.

At my granny's house, Laurel and Hardy films were on the television every other Saturday morning. I can't remember the film, but Stan Laurel and Oliver Hardy sat by a well, plucking feathers from a chicken. Whatever the movie, the film slipped into the background as if the sound was gradually turned down on the outside world.

My granny Harkin was the entry point into a distant but now familiar cinematic world. The emotion in her voice, speaking about the laughter in the cinema, made me look at my grandmother differently. She was back to her earlier, younger life, perhaps a reminder of my grandfather, who she had met in a cinema in the 1920s. Her connection to cinema from the 1920s and '30s, that emotional connection, was still there sixty years later. Perhaps, sitting with her and hearing her stories about watching Buster Keaton and Charlie Chaplin films, stoked the fire within me, my love of cinema.

Part Two

Searching for Cinematic Role Models

Light some candles and fire on the CD with the whale sounds – it's about to get deep. This book is about building endangered aspects of our inner selves – the building blocks of our character; for me, these building blocks were confidence and identity.

The "why" was undoubtedly an escape from bullying and my search for an identity. When I began my enrolment in cinema therapy, the "how" was sitting with my granny watching films, exploring a new cinematic world. Whereas my granny had Johnny Weissmuller as Tarzan and Rudolph Valentino as screen heroes, this next part is when I took command of the remote control a bit more and searched for my own cinematic role models.

It was not merely a tale of turn the TV on and slap a random film on. You have to find films, characters and narratives that speak to you. A character or story that helps to build or rebuild those blocks in your character. I learned to speak with speech therapy but grew confident and found identity and a sense of belonging with my own personal course of cinema therapy.

Dr Cinema

First coined by therapists many years ago, cinema therapy is used primarily by therapists who suggest a film where an emotional or relatable narrative can open up further discussion on the therapist's "couch". On the other hand, the client or patient may mention a film in conversation which resonated and was memorable. The therapist will then discuss why the film resonated and what parts of the film, characters or story struck a chord.

In a broad sense, cinema therapy is a form of self-help, where watching movies and immersing yourself in the narrative and the characters onscreen works to heal mental health issues or trauma – a therapeutic tool for self-growth and greater understanding.

An American neuroscientist Dr Paul J. Zak, in *Why Inspiring Stories Make Us React: The Neuroscience of Narrative*, suggested that stimulating storylines can cause a release of oxytocin, a hormone in the brain which can influence our beliefs, attitudes and behaviours. Dr Zak suggests that being emotionally immersed in a film, following the story and allowing yourself to engage with the characters can trigger a change in the oxytocin hormone in your brain.

Indeed, immersing myself in cinema and becoming engrossed in the narrative stirred something within me. Emotionally immersive stories can help us see the world differently. A classic tale of a boy meeting a girl can offer insight into how to meet someone – how to react and behave. You can identify and feel inspired by martial arts superstar Bruce Lee fighting racial discrimination. The youthful Harry Potter can teach us the importance of friendship, or the cowboys in *The Magnificent Seven* can teach us the meaning of heroism.

On a deeper level, a story like the emotional trauma of losing a son, as the family goes through in the Italian drama *The Son's Room,* can be therapeutic. A family loss is something everyone will experience at some point, and not everyone has a support network of aunties, cousins and friends to support them.

Cinema has the power to evoke deep feelings; it can profoundly resonate with us. A film like *The Son's Room*, where bereavement is a central theme, can help you come to terms with your own feelings of loss, even though *The Son's Room* is fictional. Within the fictional setting, the interplay between characters is relatable as they deal with the same human emotions of shock, anger, sadness and loss.

Cinema, in general, can inspire empathy, challenge assumptions, and promote social change. It may be the Julia Roberts drama *Erin Brockovich*, the story of an environmental activist doing the right thing, or Rick in *Casablanca*, who sacrifices love for a more significant global cause.

It could be a Farrelly brothers movie or an Akira Kurosawa film, just a story, character or situation that flicks an emotional switch inside you.

License to Pretend

Unbeknownst to him, a young David had put this form of cinema therapy into practice as a young boy. Let me predict a few things first, school bullies will always exist, noisy neighbours will always exist and that pair of jeans we all hold on to at the back of the wardrobe will never fit you again. During my formative years at school, I found bullying to be the standard playground ritual. At school, when the other children would be frustrated with me for not pronouncing words correctly or sometimes just refusing to speak, I was fully aware that it would lead to name-calling, leading me to lose self-confidence and self-esteem.

As a child with learning difficulties, silent films offered me a simpler world. Maybe my granny's memory of those days at the cinema, watching *The Gold Rush* and *The General,* forced me to stare harder at the screen and open my heart and imagination to the characters and stories that attracted her years ago. Perhaps it was that most silent films soaked in beautiful monochrome were so unlike the world we all inhabit.

Whatever the case, my switch got flicked. Watching Buster Keaton's films was where I first found some inspiration and began to re-model myself. Within social learning theory, psychologist Albert Bandura points out that human behaviour can be learned observationally by somebody else through modelling. By observing other people, we form an idea of new behaviour.

Like Harold Lloyd and Charlie Chaplin from the same period, these silent clowns were the kings of silent comedy, and I would mimic and mirror the silent comedy king Buster Keaton and fall into a phase of pretending I was a mime. I connected and mirrored visual humour simply because I imagined the world entirely visually, perhaps imagining a funnier world like a silent comedy, where bullies never had the last laugh.

Finding school so difficult, I searched for a role model and became fully immersed in Buster Keaton. Trying to amuse or distract the other children, I would pull faces, fall over and perform a silly walk – anything to move the situation on, anything that would help disguise the fact that I had difficulty with speech.

In the 1990s, Robert P. Craig, in a journal called *The Face We Put On: Carl Jung for Teachers*, discussed Swiss psychiatrist Carl Jung, and points to Jung's ideas of the "persona" and the masks we all wear. Essentially this had become my mask; my persona was to become a clown, something to hide behind – and it worked.

Being unable to speak and having communication challenges, Buster Keaton's visual world permitted me to express myself with comedy gestures and practical jokes.

Carry On Thunderballs

Going out for a walk, watching a spectator sport, playing a video game or just talking to the postman can break the stress of life. My son, David, finds his respite with video games, my friend Marty finds his respite watching football and my wife, Golda, finds her break from life with comedies like *Vacation* and *Hobson's Choice*.

Comedy films are supposed to be uplifting and funny – broad comedy films, in particular, can be the go-to movies when we need to cheer up after a bad day. It could be *Dumb and Dumber*, *Johnny English Reborn* or *The Return of the Pink Panther*, just any comedy that lightens the day.

Take the *Carry On* series, with comedy stars Sid James, Jim Dale, Joan Sims and Kenneth Williams. We see likeable yet broad characters in a series of comedy adventures. A comedy series that produced over thirty films, with the same actors – and even the same jokes, some might say. I found refuge in the *Carry On* films because of the time capsule element – the dated clothes and seaside postcard humour – a world we recognise but with one foot in a fantasy world.

No Time to Give Up

As I struggled to speak and meet new people at school, positive and fun role models onscreen helped me through each crappy day at my crappy secondary school. The zany antics of the Marx Brothers proved the perfect remedy, a departure from the day-to-day struggle of school bullies. Just watching their films reminded me to laugh a little bit more.

The Marx Brothers were actual brothers, each adopting a stage name. Adolph (later Arthur) became the harp-obsessed Harpo; Leonard became the wisecracking "Italian" Chico; Herbert became the smooth-talking Zeppo; and Julius became Groucho, the fast-talking wordsmith with his stooped walk, painted moustache, large cigar and distinctive glasses.

The brothers made their names in vaudeville before transitioning to motion pictures, just as talking pictures became a phenomenon to eager cinemagoers in the late 1920s and early 1930s. My granny Harkin had watched the Marx Brothers for the first time in the 1930s and was a first-generation fan – a link for me to the past. Having worked as a cleaner at a local cinema, she would talk about going to the cinema in the 1930s, where there would be a café serving tea where everyone would discuss the film amidst the daily gossip.

She told me how a night at the cinema was a "big night", where there would be a newsreel, a cartoon, a B-film or a serial with *Flash Gordon*, the night ending with a screening of a Marx Brothers' film, like *Horse Feathers* or *Duck Soup*. It all sounded brilliant.

The Marx Brothers were a common reference point in our house. Groucho's zippy one-liners, the outlandish situations and the memorable songs echoed around the house. During the 1930s, the Marx Brothers' verbal dexterity, particularly from Groucho, was well-timed for introducing sound to motion pictures, as were the brothers' comedy hijinks in an America suffering from The Great Depression.

When I watched the Marx Brothers films, I wished I had the confidence to utilise Groucho's zippy one-liners to disarm or distract bullies. In the Marx Brothers' films, Groucho was brilliant in stifling a bully's bad behaviour and an authority figure's pomposity. As a child, Harpo, the silent clown, was the most endearing brother; he was a bridge between the silent era of screen comedy and the new, fresher comedy films of the 1930s. I would re-watch the movies repeatedly, only to be woken by a television full of fuzzy snow. It was a cathartic experience. Harpo made me feel less alone at school. I felt a connection to Harpo's silent world.

Other less comedic cinematic screen role models during this period of teenage uncertainty, would be in the shape of the resourceful Captain Mallory in *The Guns of Navarone* or the flawed heroic character of Captain Scott in *Scott of the Antarctic*. These films of survival and endurance meant a lot to me – characters who could overcome difficult situations and any challenge that life could throw at them.

No doubt, due to the release of the rubbish ITV Sherlock Holmes series featuring Jeremy Brett, I found my most intellectual onscreen role model with Basil Rathbone as the perfect screen incarnation of Sherlock Holmes. Rathbone had starred in fourteen Holmes films, each offering a copious amount of adventure, humour, and mystery. As a young child, I was called a "spa" or a "spastic" daily. So, as I struggled to speak and appear confident at school, characters like Sherlock Holmes embodied intelligence and deductive reasoning, as Holmes would solve spy codes and get mixed up with Nazis. He was someone you could look up to – admire his intellect.

I could see in Rathbone's Holmes the wheels turning, his mind thinking over the clues of the crime. Rathbone's depiction of Holmes helped me; he was super-smart and could solve any crime. But that wasn't just it. It was the notion that Sherlock Holmes was aloof, appearing not to care. Holmes was above it. I wanted the same thing, the feeling that being called names didn't affect me, that I could rise above it.

For me, hiding behind Sherlock Holmes did help; using a pretence of cunning and intelligence helped me get through another terrible day at school. Sherlock Holmes helped because at school, dealing with communication challenges, I existed within that context of "can't speak properly", "can't think properly". No one at secondary school understood that ability is a spectrum. Even with perceived school friends, playground banter and joking can drift over the line towards where bullying begins. Classmates didn't give it enough thought; they joined the dots too quickly, believing that someone who couldn't communicate was immune from emotional pain.

If someone tells a child they are stupid or dissuades them from participating in something, thinking they're stupid or not good enough, this becomes internalised, and they begin to believe they're worthless. Comments from a judgemental teacher, who doesn't understand, can destroy ambition and confidence.

Luckily, I was escaping the culture of ignorance I felt at school by investing my imagination in cinematic role models like Sherlock Holmes, Captain Scott and James Bond.

The Man Called Bond

So now we get to the meat in this particular sandwich. My cinematic role model was simple. It had to be James Bond. My dad was a big Bond fan in the 1960s, and among my peers *Star Wars* and *Indiana Jones* only rivalled the Bond movies' popularity.

Created by Ian Fleming, James Bond first appeared in

the spy novel *Casino Royale* in 1953 and would continue to appear in many more books by other writers even after Fleming died in 1964. Fleming had always envisioned Bond transferring to the silver screen, even writing a 150-page film treatment in 1956 for his novel *Moonraker*. Yet, no film studios were interested in Fleming's ideas for a *Moonraker* film. Nevertheless, Bond finally reached the big screen when Albert R. "Cubby" Broccoli and Harry Saltzman formed Eon Productions in the early 1960s, launching the Bond series with *Dr. No* in 1962.

Bond has been around for a long time, surviving many changes in culture and audience expectations. Like all films, Bond films are a product of their time, like someone holding a social mirror reflecting the period in which they were made. For example, the first time we see Bond in *Dr. No*, a cigarette hangs from his mouth, yet when Pierce Brosnan came around to Bond in the 1990s, smoking had (rightly) become a "filthy habit" in *Tomorrow Never Dies*.

Bond is part of our cultural psyche; you only have to wear a tuxedo or hold a white cat. Bond surrounds our notions of what a spy is, our concept of masculinity and the definition of cool.

The first time I saw Bond onscreen was in the film *Octopussy*, with Roger Moore in his sixth outing as 007 – a grand spectacle of adventure, high-octane stunts, and glamorous locations. Contrary to this, I remember seeing *Never Say Never Again* next –an unofficial Bond offering from producer Kevin McClory, released the same year as *Octopussy*.

Starring original Bond Sean Connery in a dodgy wig, *Never Say Never Again* (a remake of the earlier Bond film

Thunderball) was dreadful, not even qualifying as a guilty pleasure. The dire theme song by Lani Hall is terrible, as is the sub-jazz film score by French composer Michel Legrand. It was a pale imitation of a Bond film, a forgery, a fake, with *Never Say Never Again*'s central "action" sequence involving three cars and a cautious James Bond wearing a motorcycle helmet.

Yet, my youthful analysis of *Octopussy* and *Never Say Never Again* stirred my passion for Bond. I immediately felt ownership of the character. *Never Say Never Again* intruded into *Octopussy*'s perfect glossy world that lifted my imagination and psyche away from the drab corridors and daily punishment that secondary school offered.

When I saw *Octopussy*, it felt like an event, brimming with thrilling set pieces and a relaxed and confident performance from Roger Moore. There was no "Battle of the Bonds" as the press had drummed up with the release of *Never Say Never Again*, but more of a surrender, an understanding that you need more than Sean Connery to make an actual Bond film.

Spending every weekend at my grandmother's, I had the chance to watch many Bond films as they were always on at peak time on a Saturday night, with each exciting adventure helping to grow my confidence. It was inspiring to see someone so self-confident; Bond seemed bulletproof.

During the Christmas holidays in the early 1990s, ITV screened the network premiere of *A View to a Kill*. Crowded with advertisements, the film still made an impression, with an older Roger Moore in a standout performance in his final Bond outing. Nothing could come between you and the television when a Bond film was on. Even watching an old Connery Bond film, a thirty-year-old film on the old gogglebox was appointment viewing. The juxtaposition of school life with Bond's glamorous world of fast cars and pretty girls in movies like *You Only Live Twice* or *A View to a Kill* was jarring. Yet, watching these films was a bolt for freedom, a different mindset – Bond's world fed my imagination.

Moore, much Moore

I grew up during the Roger Moore/Timothy Dalton period (and Connery, if you include his '80s stinker *Never Say Never Again*). Although without question, my three brothers and I always enjoyed the more colourful Roger Moore films, like *Moonraker* and *Octopussy*.

Moore, a star since the 1950s with *Ivanhoe*, had also played the smooth gentleman–adventurer Simon Templar in the popular 1960s series *The Saint*, so it's no surprise that Moore became the third big-screen James Bond.

Far from any spy penned by John le Carré and a departure from Connery's 60s Bond, Moore's Bond, full of English charm, a twinkle in his eye and a quip only seconds away, was so self-assured when skiing off cliffs or skydiving without a parachute. Moore was charm personified, a departure from real life.

Minus the death-defying stunts, this departure is what I needed, a role model who wasn't bothered about external forces and who was self-confident and commanding. During high unemployment, the Vietnam War and the Three-Day Week, Moore's Bond films were as much an escape for moviegoers in the 1970s as they would be for me, years later, during my troubled school years. Bond's ability to overcome any obstacle and get out of any tricky situation made such an impression on me.

He was self-reliant, composed in his thought processes and worldly wise.

Never Say Connery Again

Most people can relate to that person, musician or film character that isn't mainstream. Someone who's on the outside looking in. Around 1992, around the thirtieth anniversary of James Bond's first big-screen outing, a few more Bond films were on television, and I looked forward to seeing *On Her Majesty's Secret Service*, one Bond film I hadn't seen.

Starring an Australian model and ex-car dealer, George Lazenby was not Sean Connery, Roger Moore or any other actor who has ever played James Bond. Lazenby sprang from outside the acting fraternity, the British film industry and Europe. He was a literal outsider.

In *On Her Majesty's Secret Service*, this new Bond falls in love, marries Teresa "Tracy" di Vicenzo, and pursues arch-nemesis Ernst Stavro Blofeld (Telly Savalas) in the Swiss Alps. Diana Rigg bagged the vital role of Tracy, Bond's wife, adding a touch of gravitas to the part – perhaps cast to balance Lazenby's apparent lack of acting chops.

Legend has it that Lazenby bluffed his way into the role, using a Savile Row suit that Sean Connery never collected, with Lazenby securing the part when he punched out a stuntman during a screen test.

At any rate, watching *On Her Majesty's Secret Service* in

1992, John Barry's soundtrack and Lazenby's performance were the best things about the film. George Lazenby presented a more vulnerable Bond, a bit more human than Connery's iconic yet armour-plated Bond.

Barring Barry Nelson's attempt as "Jimmy Bond" in *Casino Royale*, an American television effort from the 1950s, Sean Connery created the role of Bond onscreen and, for many, is the ultimate James Bond. However, Lazenby offered a more human Bond for the period, with a decent slice of Sixties groove.

I think I was drawn to George Lazenby as he was an outsider who challenged convention. It's a shame that Lazenby never continued in the role; he was a great Bond. Once I learned of Lazenby's tale and how he became Bond, it made a big impression on me, and his solo outing as Bond remains a favourite.

Past Raker

Even though we travel on the same road, our experience of the journey can be different. Some people may have enjoyed attending St Peter's, but I certainly didn't. After the school was knocked down in favour of some much-needed social housing, I had a chance encounter with a fellow inmate.

He asked me how I felt about the school getting knocked down. I searched his eyes, looking for a glimmer of sarcasm. I paused and paused some more. I needed to figure out how to answer and ultimately never did answer his question.

Even though I had left school fifteen years earlier, seeing that random ex-pupil in the street made me realise that the past was still me. What happened to me at the school did happen. I can't change it, but it is over. What I have learned is that looking back, you'll see the past events in your life are dotted together, that the past is still you. It is now a part of you. The initial raw pain might have passed, but the strength gained from overcoming it now empowers.

A therapist told me once about soul recapture – a process when you try and connect the dots and recapture the essence of your inner self, like collecting a piece of your past to feel better about your present state of being. It's an internal process where I remember or re-watch the cinematic heroes who made an impression on my younger self. Heroes that stayed with me throughout childhood – connecting back to my younger self, to the heroes and cinematic role models who helped me through some of the most traumatic days of my life, this process helps me internalise who I am – at the core.

Action Royale

The flipside to cinematic screen heroes, the warning of what to watch or not to watch with impressionable young minds, was strengthened early on in my mind when I was still at school. In the 1980s, action films had somewhat moved on from Bond, sophisticated spies in dinner jackets were out and bulging muscles and more violence were now en vogue. Most of my class at school were watching more adult-oriented, contemporary films like *Bloodsport* and *Tango & Cash*. In a secondary school full of boys, all pumped full of testosterone, new stars like Sylvester Stallone and Arnold Schwarzenegger had seemingly replaced Bond, with the conversations usually following the more "eighteen-rated" material – the boobs of the leading ladies and the bare arse of Van Damme.

At secondary school, in terms of the teen audience, Bond was maybe a bit too tame when *Basic Instinct* and *Disclosure* offered more than a kiss and a quick fade to black. Even when there were seemingly wall-to-wall Bond films on television, any potential friends at school had no interest in James Bond. Not when there was Sly, Bruce (Willis) and Arnie. The classroom discussion was always on the woman with the three boobs in *Total Recall* or Miguel Ferrer snorting cocaine off a redhead's cleavage in *Robocop*.

This class discourse of the three boobs in *Total Recall* would stir male testosterone levels in the classroom. It led to threats that others who didn't join the conversation were weak and not tough enough to "get it", ultimately leading to the individual being picked on for being "different".

You can Google professional shit-stirrer Mary Whitehouse if you're more interested, but there has been a long debate about young people viewing violence and its effect on behaviour. In the 1960s, when Whitehouse was learning how to stir the pot and campaign about Britain's filth in film and television, Albert Bandura's "Bobo doll" experiment demonstrated that children might learn aggression through observation, and within the last forty years, the video nasties scandal of the early 1980s, violent video games and digital peer pressure in a classroom to view violent content online all add to this long-standing debate.

After classroom screenings of *Bloodsport* and *Tango & Cash* at my secondary school, there was undoubtedly more tension and a steady growth of bullying incidents on the school bus home. Routine end-of-term films, like *Robocop*, stirred the "juices" of the classroom environment as hostile behaviour onscreen was mirrored and replicated among pupils.

I can remember the ultra-violent scene in *Robocop* when Alex Murphy gets gunned down by a group of bad guys provoking nervous laughter in the classroom. There was a space, a moment to either say nothing or succumb to peer pressure and betray your beliefs and morals and laugh at someone effectively getting bullied onscreen.

Puberty sucks for most people, with some academic research (Dr Sally Anne Duke amongst others) suggesting that with puberty leading to higher testosterone levels in male adolescents, there may be a connection to behavioural changes such as aggression and risk-taking. At school, within a classful of male pupils going through puberty, after a classroom viewing of *In the Name of the Father*, feelings about the Northern Ireland Troubles were brought to the boil as everyone in the class became obsessed with thoughts of "blowing stuff up" and shooting protestants.

Looking back, my teachers had switched off and kept a bunch of angst-ridden pupils happy by putting on a film that would keep the class quiet.

Today, parents and teachers can make more informed choices on what movies to watch in a group environment with online reviews or this book, which you have undoubtedly already purchased at its RRP.

Nowadays, it's easier for teachers, parents and guardians to objectively analyse the content and narrative as well as checking the certification of a film, to contextualise and unpack the movie to help identify any potential problems that may arise when viewing the film in a group or family environment. A better understanding of violent content through discussion with young people or family members will also lift viewers out of the immersive bubble of watching a film. It's obvious but essential that what we view and engage with gets swallowed up in our subconscious. As James Bond gave me confidence and a sense of adventure as a young child, it makes just as much sense that a negative character in a film would provide a child with negative characteristics.

As for me, I did feel safer in the world of James Bond – a more make-believe world of good versus evil. A world that was unlike school or the tempered social environment of Northern Ireland amid a culture of bombs and bomb scares.

The Spectre of Bond

Due to legal issues after Timothy Dalton's second bite at Bond with *Licence to Kill*, there were no new Bond films during the same years I attended secondary school.

So, I relied on the appointment viewing of the yesteryear Bond flicks of Moore and Connery. There were posters, books and magazines to collect. James Bond had begun to filter into my everyday life.

Ext. Late at night, lit by the orange glow of a lamppost. I stared down at my backyard-made go-kart and thought it was the coolest thing ever. My back garden at our family home resembled the yard from *Steptoe and Son*. There would be old pram wheels, broken pieces from a chest of drawers and leaky car batteries.

Typically, I would snoop around the backyard and grab some pram wheels, the seat off a kitchen chair and a length of rope. Cue *A-Team* style montage as I pulled nails from a fence and hammered my go-kart together with a concrete brick. Like James Bond's car, first seen in *Goldfinger*, I carefully wrote DB5 onto a scrap of wood in thick white correction fluid and nailed it to the front of the go-kart. I was aware at the time, as if it were a security blanket, I had tailored Bond to my persona, which I like to call the "Bond Model".

In the words of my younger brother Barry, I had become obsessed with James Bond. Yet, in the words of psychiatrist Carl Jung, in the *Two Essays on Analytical Psychology*, I had concealed "the true nature of the individual."

I took on Bond's confidence, and it did help. Wearing a mask to protect myself made me the best version of myself. Before this "Bond Model", I had been playing the "Fool Model" à la Buster Keaton, a model I had mastered so well during my first year at secondary school.

Later at secondary school, that "fool performance", the facade, began to slip with a mix of teenage maturity and a desire for inner growth. Feeling more confident, watching Bond's world of masculinity, I changed my tactics and left the "Fool Model" behind, putting all my hopes on the Bond Model. Soon enough, with a total engagement and observation of all things Bond, the confidence and the swagger of Jimmy Bond helped a lot – a cinematic role model who fuelled my inner confidence and self-esteem.

Sky Ball

Before joining that horrible secondary school, during that summer in 1990, I did briefly find role models in other areas. I stayed with my dad in my grandmother's house, and black and white films got switched to football one summer.

Even though they had qualified for Euro '88, after years of being the "nearly men", continually being pipped to the post in qualification for the World Cup, the Republic of Ireland football team made it to Italia '90, their first football World Cup.

Suddenly, in a culture where everyone in Northern Ireland is obsessed with being British, Irish or Northern Irish, this World Cup helped me and many of my peers identify with being more Irish.

Looking back, it felt like the longest summer of childhood as Sinéad O'Connor's 'Nothing Compares 2 U' played relentlessly on car radios, there was World Cup fever as the Republic of Ireland football team took the nation on a rollercoaster ride of excitement, joy and pride. But, when asked who my favourite player was, a childhood nickname would outstay its welcome. As I could not pronounce McGrath, the surname of Irish legend Paul McGrath, I said "McGa", and it stuck and became a name I loathed. It was an annoying reminder of my inability to speak correctly.

I had never heard of Cameroon before Italia '90, and I found it inspiring that this footballing nation of Indomitable Lions roared in the face of the tournament favourites England in their quarter-final battle.

Cameroon caused a sensation, with Cameroonian striker Roger Milla becoming a fun role model during that hot summer in 1990. Aged thirty-eight years old, Milla scored four goals at Italia '90, giving the world an iconic goal celebration as he ran to a corner flag and danced with joy. It was inspiring.

Before the World Cup, I wasn't the biggest football fan, having found the cinema far too appealing. This was the era before billion-pound companies fought over the rights to broadcast football on television, and, barring the FA Cup final each year, it felt like a live football match was rarely on the box. So as an eleven-year-old, Italia '90 made a big impression.

You haven't accidentally skipped a chapter or had a stroke; this was a temporary deviation in my search for cinematic role models. This left turn into that warm summer of football in 1990 underlines the importance that positive role models can be found in unlikely places.

A Quantum of Wisdom

When I was in secondary school, it was the tale of two classroom experiences – where a teacher sat at one end of a room, and pupils sat at the other end; in the same space but operating in different worlds. School back then was a million miles away in their awareness of pupils of colour, disability and LGBTQ+ than any average school today.

Today, working in the education sector, I have seen first-hand how teachers and classroom assistants approach children with special educational needs. Today there is much more "between-desk-teaching", where teachers move around the room, allowing themselves to become more available to the pupil, helping to monitor and support each pupil. There's more awareness, more acknowledgement of difference and ultimately more kindness.

Yet, I have also seen in some schools that, let's say, are more academically obsessed. Young people are pushed and pushed to get the grades – made to zero in on achieving the best possible grade. Ultimately putting too much pressure on young shoulders.

In terms of special educational needs, every school needs to offer an equality of opportunity to every pupil, with a focus on reducing the stigma of being "different". At some schools, a young person with special educational needs can become the proverbial thorn in the school's faculty. "We're not a school that caters for those children", "We don't have funding for more staff" – if that's the case, you are not inclusive enough.

On Your Personal Computer Service

Today, every young person seems to have a mobile phone, or what it really is, a portable computer, as no one ever seems to use it to make phone calls. Keeping up with your Instagram posts or having an active online presence can add stress to your life. Or just that pit-of-the-stomach feeling that you're the only person in your year group that's not online with a photo of yourself at McDonald's, or you're the only one in class without the latest iPhone tucked away in your schoolbag.

I often hear; "It's bad enough I'm in school for six hours, only to be reminded about it for the next four hours when I get home". I'm paraphrasing, but I often hear a version of the above statement when discussing such online learning platforms like Google Classroom – the constant dinging on their mobile device about homework deadlines adding daily anxiety.

Not so many years ago, bullying usually ended at the school gates or on the bus home. Nowadays, with social media, life is typically recorded, posted and shared, regardless of how boring or exciting the event happens to be. A bully can access what a home and a family look like and see their photos and videos posted on social media. Without the proper support, bullying could potentially never end. If anything, the need for more role models is more important than ever.

Fashion, youth language, technology and culture can change, but young people are still young. They are still insecure about their identity, wonder who their real friends are, sell chewing gum in their locker rooms and write suggestive words on the bog walls. So even with a change in system, awareness and culture, teenage angst remains and, with that in mind, so does the need for role models.

As for me, looking back over forty years, being a non-verbal child I faced the challenges of learning to speak. In hindsight, the emotional scarring of being an unwanted child by my biological parents and my subsequent adoption left me emotionally detached.

Looking at the screen and seeing a cinematic hero, such as James Bond, must have been an outlet for this trauma. So, from a personal standpoint, I am certain that cinematic role models helped develop my confidence, identity and worldview regarding relationships and family politics.

Essentially, I had my day with James Bond. It was there when I needed it, and now when I watch *On Her Majesty's Secret Service* or *Goldfinger*, I'm not merely watching old films; I'm reliving old memories. Bond now belongs to someone else who needs diversion and inspiration from everyday life.

Part Three

Cinematic role models and young people

I hated being a teenager, and if you had read the other chapters and weren't flicking through this book at a charity shop, you will have read why I had such a bad time as a young person at school.

Seeing the world as an adolescent is a search for identity, expectations and hope in an ever-changing world of technology and awareness of gender. There is enormous social pressure to have the latest phone and live a second life on social media. One such young person attending one such group session on "social media expectations" had no interest in social media. However, they "still felt FOMO" (fear of missing out) that everyone was at the party except them.

Naturally, unless you're a robot, these pressures lead to poor self-esteem. Schools, parents and social services offer solutions, and if social media becomes too much, simple actions like a digital detox or a walk in the rain can help.

There was no such thing as social media when I was at school, and although there were plenty of rainy days growing up in Ireland, there was no need for a walk in it. During my difficult and troubling experiences at school, a roll call of onscreen role models and a belief in cinema therapy made me believe in myself. I could shelve my doubts, anxieties and worries.

As an informal educator, I engage with young people on media projects and discuss films that inspire them. I learn from them about their screen heroes, the cinematic role models in the twenty-first century who encourage them. Some of these heroes are TikTok stars or YouTube sensations, a memorable song or a new trend or an inspiring Instagram story. Even though these heroes can be fleeting, they serve their purpose if they inspire others and encourage people to overcome obstacles and daily stresses and worries.

Some of these heroes can be found in gaming, where a young person switches off the stress of life, switches on a video game and escapes into the world of *Super Mario*. In 2023, BBC journalist Andrew Rogers reported on the importance of escapism when playing the video game *Zelda*. The online article discusses how *The Legend of Zelda: Breath of the Wild* in particular has helped young people navigate difficult emotions, escape life and even cope with bereavement, and how video games have helped "neurodivergent players to feel more comfortable to make connections" with other people.

Although he's not a fan of *Zelda*, my son David, who copes with stress daily at school, comes home and switches off life and switches on the world of *Super Mario*.

David lets his mind be distracted and finds a different, fun world where he makes positive choices.

Whether in the digital world of Snapchat or the real world of school bullies and teenage anxiety, film characters and stories can alleviate pressure on young people. Turning down the lights, switching off social media or the world outside your living room window can help. The bright screen of a cinema or television, with the sound of another world encircling you, can transport you to another mental state – a positive state of mind, where life takes a break and Bond or Batman takes over.

Like me, some young people develop an interest in cinema with the help and influence of a parent, sibling or grandparent. Many young people may learn about a new film the old-fashioned way simply by word of mouth or from suggestions from a streaming service guided by algorithms. As I usually try to collaborate with young people on filmmaking, cinema is the most common medium discussed.

When working with a group of young people, establishing a free-flowing, open session permits the young person, when figuring out ideas for a film project, to have more freedom to express themselves and what is important to them in their own world. This allows the young person to grow in confidence and to offer up some suggestions about the type of films they find stimulating or interesting.

Some films, like *The Danish Girl*, might connect to any young person who is curious about their gender. This relatable narrative may lead to a meaningful discussion about a sensitive area of their life. Other films are those larger-than-life films, like *Transformers*, which provide a respite – a power down from real life. Or it could be a relatable drama, like *Wonder*, that helps answer an insecure feeling or doubt.

Wherever their interest in cinema comes from, I listened, and what follows is some of those films discussed during the last fifteen years of working with young people. Films that have floated around on late-night television or used to fill up the schedule on a Sunday afternoon. So, who better to start with than Alfred Hitchcock and *Stage Fright*.

A feminine icon who challenged gender, conquered Hollywood and became a model for sophistication

German-born Marlene Dietrich was a role model, light years ahead of her time. She was vocal about her homeland and the rise of Nazism, refusing to support or participate in Nazi propaganda. Dietrich spoke candidly about her sexuality, having male and female lovers, and in 1930 famously kissed a woman onscreen in Josef von Sternberg's *Morocco*.

In Alfred Hitchcock's *Stage Fright*, Marlene Dietrich played Charlotte Inwood and instructed the crew where to place the camera and lights during production. Dressed in glamorous furs and pearls, Dietrich's presence in *Stage Fright* adds a certain frisson to the character of Charlotte Inwood.

Stage Fright begins promisingly, as a safety curtain reveals a London ravaged by war. Jane Wyman plays Eve, who hides her friend Jonathan (Richard Todd), a man accused of murdering the husband of Charlotte Inwood (Marlene Dietrich). In order to spy on Charlotte, Eve poses as her maid. However, Eve's emotions and actions begin to become muddled as she falls in love with Inspector Wilfred "Ordinary" Smith (Michael Wilding), the chief investigator into the murder of Charlotte Inwood's husband.

Stage Fright was a return to England for Hitchcock, if not a return to form after the misfire of *Under Capricorn* the previous year. Produced after the box office failures of *Rope* and *Under Capricorn*, *Stage Fright* is another exciting film from Hitchcock, helped by an alluring performance from Marlene Dietrich, one of the screen's most incredible role models.

"One day, Sasha asked for a dress, I was embarrassed. But I saw the look in the mirror, with the dress. Such happiness. And I didn't care what people thought anymore"

I had never heard of gender dysphoria. Not until a young person told me about conversations with teachers at school. This young person felt depressed and confused about their gender identity and sex. They felt anxious and had already spoken to doctors, parents and a social worker. So, frustrated with life, this particular young person felt that they needed a sense of belonging, a sense of acceptance.

So, I suggested an engaging film by seasoned LGBTQ+ filmmaker Sebastien Lifshitz. *Little Girl* is a French-language documentary film with beautiful cinematography and a touching family story about a vulnerable young child. Born as a male at birth, Sasha felt she was a girl before the age of four, and the documentary follows her in the bubble of her parent's protection and the unkindness of the outside world.

Little Girl is an interesting and emotional documentary. However, as we follow Sasha's story, the documentary suggests more questions than answers as it brushes over controversial topics like puberty blockers, focusing much of its glare on Sasha's protective and caring parents. But what did the young person think?

They did watch the film and enjoyed learning about Sasha's family trying to understand their child's feelings, although they did feel that the documentary was only "from the mother's point of view." Regardless of my critique of the film, for the young person I was conversing with, *Little Girl* lifted some of their anxiety and allowed them to believe they were not alone in their thoughts and feelings about identity and gender.

A Trip to the Moon

When the film is older than your grandad, it becomes easy to poke holes in a leaky storyline. Yet, with over a hundred and twenty years of history, cinema has much to offer – so let's look at the oldest film on this list.

In 2012, when I was explaining film history to a community group, I screened *A Trip to the Moon*, a classic from the early days of cinema, made way back in 1902. The group at the community centre was comprised mainly of young people with special educational needs; some had ADHD (attention deficit hyperactivity disorder) and others had emotional and mental health needs.

With its hand-painted frames, *A Trip to the Moon* was a pleasing sensory experience many in the group enjoyed. *A Trip to the Moon* has memorable visuals and, as it is under fifteen minutes in length, it gave the group a more profound understanding of the story.

I had first watched the film as a child, but years passed before I saw it again as a restored version on YouTube. Jam-packed with inventive special effects and charming visuals, *A Trip to the Moon* concerns a daring expedition to the Moon, where a group of brave explorers battle with alien inhabitants.

The film starts after a short briefing sequence as our intrepid explorers blast into space, land on the Moon's surface and observe the Earth rising into the night sky, with everyone seemingly able to survive the Moon's environment without using spacesuits. Just as one of the explorers' umbrellas morphs into a seven-foot mushroom, our hopeful explorers meet monkey-like inhabitants. Yes, it's bananas.

The director of *A Trip to the Moon*, Georges Méliès, is an important figure in film history, heavily influencing science fiction as a genre whilst pioneering early cinematic techniques such as multiple exposures and hand-painted frames. Méliès was the original auteur of world cinema and had a massive studio built in Paris with a glass roof to allow natural light to film his mini masterpieces.

In 2011 Martin Scorsese directed the excellent family film *Hugo*, a Dickensian tale of a young, orphaned boy who meets a grumpy Georges Méliès at a Paris train station. Starring, among many others, Chloë Grace Moretz, Jude Law and Sacha Baron Cohen, *Hugo* is a love letter from Scorsese to Méliès and the early life of cinema and its creators. It's a great film, with great performances, slick-looking CGI and some lovely flashbacks of Méliès producing his beautiful films with magnificent effects and costumes.

Anyhow, in a word, well, a couple of words – *A Trip to the Moon* is a triumph of early cinema. The glorious image of the Moon's face, with the explorers' bullet-shaped rocket nestled in one of its eyes is one of cinema's greatest and most famous images.

The King of Comedy

Another film I screened for the same group, and I had watched at a similar age, was *The General*. A silent film from the 1920s, where I found Buster Keaton's clowning a perfect foil for bullies and an early role model. Johnnie (Buster Keaton) has two loves in life: his train, "The General", and his sweetheart Annabelle Lee (Marion Mack). Told with intertitles to help explain the plot, union spies steal Johnnie's train, a train on which Johnnie's beloved Annabelle is a passenger, with Johnnie doing his best to save his girl and his train.

There are two fantastic chases involving a string of stunts as Keaton sits on the front of the train's cowcatcher, falls off a Boneshaker bicycle, and runs along the top of a train. One iconic stunt is Keaton sitting on a coupling rod of a train, only realising his predicament as the train enters a tunnel. Filmed on location in Oregon in the summer of 1926, *The General* was ground-breaking, the stunt work extraordinary and the comedic performance of Buster Keaton breath-taking. No mugging or big gestures, Keaton, the man with the big eyes and stone-wall face, allows his deadpan expression to tell Johnnie's story.

In his personal life, Keaton loved trains, and in one sequence, there is the staging of a real train crashing into a riverbed. If you compare the train chase in Alfred Hitchcock's *Number 17*, produced six years later in 1932, full of poor rear-projection and model trains, *The General* is a clear winner. Filmed on the 23rd of July 1926, the train running off the bridge in *The General* is the most expensive stunt in silent film history, costing $42,000. It still looks fantastic, and if you couldn't be bothered watching *The General* from start to finish, the scene of the train running off the bridge is available on YouTube.

Buster Keaton was a true auteur of silent cinema, a master technician and a comedy pioneer. Certainly, Keaton was much more interested in cinematic technique than his contemporary clowns (Chaplin and Lloyd). Yet, *The General* was met with mixed reviews during its original release, with Keaton's subsequent move to MGM leaving the gifted director with little creative control.

Nevertheless, *The General* is a must-see film, with a perfect running time of just under eighty minutes. It's hilarious and fast-paced, with beautiful black-and-white photography and striking visuals. It's suitable for all ages, with text appearing sporadically onscreen to help explain the story, a joyous experience from the first frame – a comedy masterclass.

"The future of Narnia rests on your courage"

It's always fantastic to hear about the screen heroes that young people look up to, like Buzz Lightyear, Wonder Woman or the screen heroine Katniss Everdeen from the *Hunger Games* franchise. After many years of working with groups and facilitating film or media programs, I have heard and listened to many suggestions regarding fictional characters where young people find inspiration, confidence or distraction from everyday life.

Often, these suggestions are larger-than-life characters – Marvel heroes or films they watched as a younger child, which possibly planted a seed and bore a deep connection. Through many conversations, it has become clear that some of the movies mentioned have become more important as a particular child has matured through adolescence. During that latter half of the school year, when exams are looming in the near distance, a familiar film may offer a diversion, a respite or even a reminder of a less stressful time.

When working with young people on video and film projects, I have often found that allowing their imagination to stretch to its potential and "playing out" their dreams with creative role-playing can be therapeutic. A young person can take on a new identity, allowing them to practice different behaviours within their personality, as well as helping to combat stress and anxiety. This approach is beneficial when the ideas addressed in a brainstorming session mention a fantasy environment.

As a child, I had never paid much attention to *The Chronicles of Narnia: The Lion, the Witch and the Wardrobe*. Based on the novel by C. S. Lewis, I remember watching the BBC adaptation in the 1980s, which probably passed an hour on a Sunday evening but didn't make an impression.

Anyway, in 2005, an enjoyable, if not overlong, version of the story was released. Only needing a large cupboard to parody the film, young people acted out a scene from the movie during a group session, their imagination driving the ideas. Everyone in the group enjoyed just taking on a new identity and pretending to be someone else for a short time.

In the film, in contrast to the magical world of Narnia, there's the real-life, real-world situation of a group of four young siblings sent off to a large house in the country to escape the death and destruction of a bombing raid during the Second World War. Bored, the children find a wardrobe that transports them to Narnia's fairy-tale world. Unlike the real-life historical events of the Second World War, this fantasy world has talking animals and God-like lions.

Although I found some of *The Lion, the Witch and the Wardrobe* a bit overlong, I could see why those young people in my group enjoyed it. In the real world of a war-torn Europe in the 1940s, the four children, little Lucy (Georgie Henley), big sister Susan (Anna Popplewell) and their two brothers Peter (William Moseley) and Edmund (Skandar Keynes), have no control over what happens to them. But in this fantasy world beyond the wardrobe, they find empowerment and are the masters of their destinies.

Although the shots of the four siblings walking through the snow with their furry coats look like a John Lewis advert, *The Lion, the Witch and the Wardrobe* is a well-crafted family film with brave young heroes and an evil witch, perfect for pre-teens, if not a little long in the running time. Produced in the wake of *Harry Potter* and *The Lord of the Rings*, this type of big-screen fantasy was very much en vogue, and, like most big-budget fantasies, there are a couple of sequels. Even when "The Professor", played by Jim Broadbent, runs Peter Cushing's *Doctor Who* a close second in the dotty old man sweepstakes, *The Lion, the Witch and the Wardrobe* is still very enjoyable and well worth checking out.

> "And remember, my sentimental friend, that a heart is not judged by how much you love, but by how much you are loved by others"

Christmas promises many things: plum puddings, unwanted gifts and drunken in-laws. Among the many positive things, Christmas offers a yuletide screening of *The Wizard of Oz*. A young GCSE student who enjoyed many fantasy films, including *Fantastic Beasts: The Secrets of Dumbledore* – thanks to an elderly family member who tapped into their interest in fantasy films – introduced them to the intergenerational classic *The Wizard of Oz*. In this young person's mind, these fantasy films suggested another world, an opportunity to turn off "real life".

The Wizard of Oz is a grade-A escapist film that can develop positive mental health and well-being, as cinema has the power to help viewers recuperate from the stresses of modern life. As told to me, this young person just wanted "to do nothing" after a week with his head in an algebra book. They didn't want to work any harder than just sitting with their family and forgetting the outside world for two hours.

The Wizard of Oz enjoyed plenty of airtime as young people discussed Dorothy Gale's (Judy Garland) grey and dull world of a Kansas farm and her hope for a world over the rainbow. Beginning in black and white (dipped in sepia), for anyone who doesn't know the story, a dramatic tornado sends Dorothy and her dog Toto to the land of Oz. Once there, Dorothy enters a world seeped in glorious Technicolor. On her way up the yellow brick road, Dorothy meets a Scarecrow (Ray Bolger) that needs a brain, a Tin Man (Jack Haley) who needs a heart and a Cowardly Lion (Bert Lahr).

In the original script, the character of Dorothy was initially to remain in black and white, with the world of Oz in Technicolor. Her character would stay black and white until the Good Witch (Billie Burke) tapped her with her magic wand, resulting in Dorothy turning to colour with the rest of the film. Ultimately, this proved too difficult; nevertheless, the quintessential family film remains.

The balance between childhood innocence, optimism and desire has never resonated more with young and old than Judy Garland's rendition of 'Somewhere Over the Rainbow'. Sung beautifully, with the grey skies behind Dorothy, this classic song perfectly sets up the magical world that awaits Dorothy and the audience.

The glorious Technicolor is matched by the wide-eyed, childlike quality of Judy Garland's marvellous performance as Dorothy. Dorothy is an excellent role model, offering excellent teamwork and leadership skills. She was determined to lead her newfound friends to the Emerald City and was also considerate of the needs of her small team. It's no wonder that the film struck such a chord with audiences for generations. The fantasy milieu surrounding Dorothy, the memorable dialogue, the themes and the imagery are all marvellous. It's a timeless classic that offers a colourful world filled with flying monkeys, talking trees and the simple truth that the enjoyment and love for *The Wizard of Oz* will last forever.

"I've lived a lot of lives... But I'm done running from my past"

Introduced in *Iron Man 2* more than a decade ago and amid multiple COVID-19 delays and plenty of bit parts in other Marvel films, Natasha Romanoff, aka Black Widow, finally gets her origin story in an impressive Marvel effort from director Cate Shortland.

As every Marvel fan knows, Natasha (Scarlett Johansson) has no future, so the narrative gives her a past. We begin her origin story in the 1990s, with Natasha as a young child living with her Soviet sleeper family in America. The story jumps ahead two decades. Natasha and her sister Yelena (Florence Pugh) break Dad out of prison and work together as a family to bring down cockney Russian Ray Winstone and his Red Room operation.

Recommended to me by a young person as a "different" kind of superhero film, *Black Widow* was compared to the much edgier, expletive-loaded superhero film *Logan*. I was a part-time fan of Marvel, but after seeing the lion's share of their recent output, I had begun to get bored of the repetitiveness of some of the studio's more recent flicks.

Yet, straight off the bat with *Black Widow*, you could forget you're watching a superhero film. The screenplay seizes the most common tropes of the spy genre and designs a Marvel superhero that, up until the third act, is unlike a superhero film. Akin to a much straighter action flick, there's a similarity to *On Her Majesty's Secret Service*, with a bit of business with mind-controlled women dotted worldwide and action set pieces you'd more likely see in *Mission Impossible*. Okay, it falls apart towards the end, where the screen is flush with the usual CGI shenanigans. Yet the performances are good, and the film is much more family-friendly than *Logan*.

Although, the real triumph in *Black Widow* is the family drama staged between the familiar action sequences. Natasha has a troubled past, a dysfunctional family and a lack of connection to other people. These vulnerabilities allow her to relate to a teen audience; questions about trust, family and how to fit in. It's little wonder that *Black Widow* was recommended to me; the lead characters' anxieties probably spoke to a young person's innermost thoughts. In the *Avengers*, Natasha puts on a brave face, but here, away from the group, the veil of bravado drops off, and she reveals a more melancholy demeanour.

These vulnerabilities are balanced with extraordinary strength, agility, and expertise in martial arts, empowering *Black Widow* to be a progressive character and a kick-ass superheroine. With solid performances, a healthy mix of family drama and sharing enough similarities with Marvel's established oeuvre to satisfy core fans, *Black Widow* is a solid entry in Marvel's seemingly never-ending franchise.

"There are things that will happen that make you feel powerless... and make you feel insignificant. But that's it. They're just feelings. And sometimes you have to stop feeling... (and) start doing"

When discussing potential film ideas with young people, the discussion often arrives in horror cinema. Some fake blood and spooky library music can cement ideas into a feasible project that can sometimes result in an excellent example of youth work practice.

Coming recommended to me as the submarine version of 2017's *Life*, Kristen Stewart is the lead heroine in the sci-fi thriller *Underwater*; another nature takes revenge plot as a crew of aquatic researchers gets more than their feet wet at the bottom of the ocean. Although *Underwater* was a retread of the many monster flicks that have gone before, *Underwater* was a great jumping-off point into other sci-fi films.

Influenced by Mario Bava's seminal shocker *Planet of the Vampires* is the 1979 film *Alien*, where an ensemble cast of British thesps and a (then) new screen heroine will make you believe that "In space, no one can hear you scream." In *Alien*, the story is a straightforward "old dark house" style horror, only in deep space. A dust bucket spaceship called the Nostromo is returning to Earth and intercepts "a transmission of unknown origin". After investigating the mysterious signal, a predatory alien species invades their ship.

Ellen Ripley (Sigourney Weaver), the protagonist of the first four *Alien* films, is a heroic role model – an iconic heroine who has had a lasting impression on female empowerment in popular cinema. But then, Ripley does more than survive an alien attack. She is not onboard the Nostromo as set decoration; she's not there as Captain Dallas's (Tom Skerritt) love interest. Ripley questions the motivations of other characters on the Nostromo; she questions authority – Ripley's the hero, and the film belongs to her.

The character of Ellen Ripley created a new archetype of screen heroine, where heroines such as Kristen Stewart's Norah Price in *Underwater* would soon follow.

In the first *Alien* sequel entitled *Aliens*, Ripley transforms into a motherly *Rambo* as the tense stillness of *Alien* morphs into an overblown action film. Ellen Ripley returned in two more sequels in the 1990s, with *Alien 3* returning to the "old dark house in space" template of the first film. Ripley is one of the most important protagonists in cinema history, changing the course of female representation in popular cinema – a great cinematic role model.

"I've come to believe it's not so much what you believe. It's how hard you believe it"

Based on a theme park ride, *Jungle Cruise* was eventually released after being delayed due to the COVID-19 pandemic. Set during the First World War, *Jungle Cruise*, featuring Dwayne Johnson alongside Emily Blunt as a clumsy love interest, is unashamedly old-fashioned, with a muddled story about a legendary mystical tree deep in the Amazon. As the talk on *Jungle Cruise* began to wane, the entire conversation drifted towards another franchise, which *Jungle Cruise* drew inspiration from.

After spending much of the 1970s as Hollywood's new golden boy, with a couple of box office smashes, director

Steven Spielberg ended the decade with his wartime comedy *1941*. Featuring *Saturday Night Live* favourites Dan Aykroyd and John Belushi, this lacklustre comedy was a rare misstep for such a formidable hitmaker. In need of a sure-fire hit, Spielberg and creative partner George Lucas turned to the spirit of Saturday matinee serials and created a B-movie franchise on a grand scale.

Starring Harrison Ford, the first film in the *Indiana Jones* series, *Raiders of the Lost Ark*, was an enormous success where our intrepid hero fights Nazis in a chase to recover the Ark of the Covenant. Since the series began over forty years ago, Indy has fought evil Nazis, Thuggees and deluded Russians, and in his latest entry, *Indiana Jones and the Dial of Destiny*, Indy's seemingly fighting arthritis.

The second film in the series, *Indiana Jones and the Temple of Doom*, is my favourite. Set a year before the events in *Raiders*, *Temple of Doom* begins with a Busby Berkley-stylised dance number as Indy (à la Bond in *Goldfinger*) meets nightclub singer Willie Scott (Kate Capshaw) in Club Obi Wan.

This opening sequence at Club Obi Wan, arguably the best opening in the entire series, involves a poisoned Indy searching for an antidote as Willie searches for an expensive chunk of jewellery. The action keeps coming as we meet Short Round (Ke Huy Quan), Indy's twelve-year-old sidekick, as Indy, Willie and Short Round arrive in India and search for a sacred stone stolen from a village.

Deep underneath Pankot Palace, children dig for the missing two Sankara Stones, and just as Indy has his hands on three of these sacred stones, he hears the screams of the children and delves deeper into the *Temple of Doom*...

Temple of Doom, with its human sacrifice, torture, child slavery and vivid scenes depicting black magic, is the edgier, darker film of the *Indiana Jones* series, similar to *The Empire Strikes Back* as the darker *Star Wars* entry. *Temple of Doom* is the underrated film of the series, its darkness only raising the stakes, the adventure feeling all the more dangerous than before.

The action sequences are non-stop, as Spielberg literally takes you on a rollercoaster ride as Indy, Willie and Short Round speed through a mine in a tiny cart. The customary fights, creepy crawlies, booby traps and a genuine helping of comedy woven throughout the script make *Indiana Jones and the Temple of Doom* a fun two hours.

Ke Huy Quan as Short Round is a brave young role model, saving the life of Indiana Jones and offering up a fun and engaging young hero with genuine warmth in Indy's fatherly relationship with Short Round. Indiana Jones, lifting his attire from a forgotten Charlton Heston film (*Secret of the Incas*), is a solid role model. Cultured, well-educated, courageous, funny and an expert in archaeology, ancient languages and history, Indiana Jones made education fun.

"In spite of everything. I still believe that people are really good at heart"

Anne Frank, a teenage girl hiding from the Nazis, became a symbol of the victims of the Holocaust and an international icon for her heroism and courage as she famously wrote a diary about her experiences hiding from the Nazis in occupied Amsterdam.

Anne Frank's diary, originally written in Dutch and published in 1947, is a first-hand account of life as a young Jewish girl hiding in an attic for two years during the Second World War. Directed by George Stevens, *The Diary of Anne Frank* is a tense and poignant drama – an excellent biographical film documenting the short life of a brave Jewish girl.

Beginning in Holland in 1945, Anne's father, Otto Frank (Joseph Schildkraut), slowly enters a deserted building. He finds his daughter's diary and begins to read Anne's words.

The story shifts to 1942, and we visit Anne Frank (Millie Perkins) and her life in the attic. Anne and seven other people, including her mother, father and older sister, hide in fear. Unable to make a sound during the day, the film chronicles the everyday challenges of hiding from the Nazis, the family quarrels and Anne's romance with Peter Van Daan (Richard Beymer), the son of another family who hides in the attic with Anne.

Anne Frank is a real-life role model, and the film celebrates her optimism, creativity and determination. Anne is a face to the millions of Jews killed by the Nazis during the Holocaust, and the film is a tragic story of human courage and resilience.

The performances are dramatic and heartfelt, and the black-and-white cinematography is beautiful. The action is claustrophobic, as we rarely leave the tight living quarters of Anne's living space.

The running time of three hours sucks you into Anne's world, where children must act like adults in a harrowing coming-of-age drama.

> "The future has not been written. There is no fate but what we make for ourselves"

As an educator working within film and video, I focus on how media and film reflect the advancement (or lack of) of female representation onscreen. In the lead-up to International Women's Day each year, working alongside young people, we celebrate the achievements of women worldwide and raise awareness of the ongoing struggle for equality.

During a group work session, some of our discussion began with Bette Davis and Katharine Hepburn, their film efforts from the 1940s, and more recent fare like Reese Witherspoon as sorority-queen-turned-lawyer in the charming comedy film *Legally Blonde*.

The underpinning issue in our discussion moved on to how strong female characters fit into an action film. The conversation steered towards *The Terminator*, where a cyborg is sent from the future to kill Sarah Connor, the mother of a future resistance leader – a film that's been around since the 1980s featuring a man in the lead role.

Even though Arnold Schwarzenegger takes up much of the room on the posters, Sarah Connor, played by Linda Hamilton, is the real star. Beginning her character arc as a distressed waitress, she has transformed into a kick-ass military-minded mum by the second instalment, *Terminator 2: Judgment Day*.

Terminator 3: Rise of the Machines and *Terminator Salvation* sent the franchise in another direction, before returning to the small screen with Lena Headey as Sarah Connor in *Terminator: The Sarah Connor Chronicles*.

There was a cinematic misstep with *Terminator Genisys* before Linda Hamilton returned as an older, battled-hardened Sarah in *Terminator: Dark Fate*. In this latest entry, Sarah Connor has become a more mature female icon and undoubtedly one of American action cinema's most famous female characterisations.

The franchise is a mixed bag, with the television series *Terminator: The Sarah Connor Chronicles* proving to be the worst entry, with scripts that sound like they were written by AI. Even when most of the films contain strong violence and profanity, particularly in the first two films in the series, there's no question that Sarah Connor is a quintessential cinematic role model. The fact that Sarah Connor in *Dark Fate* is now a little older, a little greyer and wiser perhaps, is even more welcome given a lack of strong, more senior female representation onscreen.

"It's not about deserve. It's about what you believe. And I believe in love"

In 2017, *Wonder Woman* breathed fresh air into the overpopulated world of the male-oriented superhero film. After a minor role in the *Fast & Furious* franchise, Gal Gadot, a former Miss Israel, transforms from model-turned-bit-player to a significant Hollywood leading lady in *Wonder Woman*.

A year earlier, Wonder Woman's debut in *Batman v Superman: Dawn of Justice* offered audiences a respite from the gloomy narrative, but now in her first solo cinematic effort, *Wonder Woman* remains as one of the best DC superhero films.

Gadot plays Diana (aka Wonder Woman), raised on the hidden, all-female island of Themyscira. Diana, along with the other leather-clad warriors, spends most of her time training in the art of war, unaware that the First World War rages on in the outside world. Steve (Chris Pine), an American pilot, crashes his plane just outside Diana's idyllic paradise, and the Amazon warriors flip through the air, shooting arrows at the invading German army.

In a sequence that will undoubtedly become iconic among fans of the DC Extended Universe, the story moves forward as Diana joins Steve in the outside world. On a First World War battlefield, Steve instructs Diana, "This is no man's land, Diana – it means no man can cross it". Refusing to stand by as people suffer, Diana jumps into action – a single female amid an army of men, striding across no man's land, leading the charge as a hail of gunfire ripples off her shield.

Under the direction of a woman for the first time, this is a superhero film that the DC Extended Universe needed. After the bloated trio of *Man of Steel*, *Batman v Superman* and *Suicide Squad*, *Wonder Woman* has a lighter approach and is more than just a good superhero film; it's a good film, period.

Director Patty Jenkins lifts a few notes from Richard Donner's *Superman: The Movie* playbook, leaving the po-faced seriousness of *Batman v Superman* behind and creating a fun, sometimes subversive comic book adventure. As the first female-led superhero in years, Diana/Wonder Woman is confident and assertive – the perfect screen heroine and role model.

"I do not stand by in the presence of evil!"

The discussion on female representation in popular cinema continued with *Alita: Battle Angel*. Directed by cult filmmaker Robert Rodriguez (*Spy Kids*) and based on a popular manga comic, *Alita: Battle Angel* is set in a futuristic city in the twenty-sixth century, with a female cyborg who kicks ass.

Young people in the discussion group thought that the special effects were "awesome" and that the main character was "cool", but no one told me what the story was about. So here it goes, set in 2563, three hundred years after a war known as "The Fall", Alita (Rosa Salazar) is a three-hundred-year-old cyborg who looks like a teenage girl.

Found abandoned and disembodied in a scrap yard by a fatherly doctor (Christoph Waltz), who's a dab hand at repairing cyborgs, the cyber doctor rebuilds her, renaming her Alita after his dead daughter. Alita has no memory, only her warrior instincts, but soon develops a crush on a teenage boy (Keean Johnson) while slowly learning about her troubled past.

It's impossible to produce this kind of science fiction film today without drawing comparisons to *Blade Runner*, *Rollerball* and the silent film classic *Metropolis*, but it's hard to ignore. Everything onscreen feels familiar, but there's still enough going on to enjoy. Special effects supremo James Cameron is behind the scenes; unsurprisingly, the motion capture effects and action sequences (when they eventually appear) in *Alita: Battle Angel* are visually impressive and thrilling.

What struck me, and perhaps the real reason why the film got the thumbs up from a group of young people, is that the main character Alita, like many young people, feels like an outsider. When a young person signs up for a new coding club or football team, some young people don't know anyone and can feel different and out of place for various reasons. Alita, loaded with many outsider and misfit characteristics, is ideal for a young person to possibly identify with and hopefully, in time, lead them to stop caring about feeling "different".

In the film, Alita is single-minded, courageous and kicks a lot of cyborg ass. She looks like a live-action anime character, literally wide-eyed as she learns of her new world. Just like your average teenager, Alita struggles with her identity and falls in love all too easily with the first person she meets. Overall, there's some clunky dialogue and a bloated running time, but enough to warrant it as a good film with striking special effects and, in Alita, a strong and brave role model.

"I've known what it is to feel lonely and helpless and to have the whole world against me, and those are things that no man or woman ought to feel"

Any movie that featured an innocent man on the run and an ice-cool blonde mixed up in an international spy ring got my attention when I searched for cinematic role models. Released in 1935, *The 39 Steps* would epitomise Alfred Hitchcock's early British period and establish the first "Hitchcock Blonde" with the casting of Madeleine Carroll as Pamela.

Borrowing little from its source, the 1915 novel by John Buchan, Hitchcock's black and white masterpiece kicks things off nicely when a mysterious gunshot breaks up a crowd during a music hall act. In the commotion, Richard Hannay (Robert Donat), a Canadian staying in London, brings a seductive female spy home to his flat and learns about a shadowy spy ring.

The following day, the mysterious spy has a knife in her back, with Hannay soon learning that he's wanted for her murder. On the run, Hannay is an innocent man, finding romance with Pamela en route to the London Palladium, where he finally learns the secret of "the 39 steps".

The 39 Steps is a cast-iron classic of British cinema, with its fast pacing and memorable set pieces, and with his matinée idol looks and weary expression, Robert Donat, in the role of Richard Hannay, is resourceful and brave; he has all the attributes you would expect from a positive role model. I was drawn towards Richard Hannay's character, as he was also an outsider, on his own, searching for answers – a charismatic cinematic role model.

"Life is up there. And life always matters"

Senior citizens and young people can sometimes find themselves on the same project. Typically, these are intergenerational projects, and ideas for possible projects can range from stilted daytime television to classic American cinema.

After a decade of creating cult television fare (*Lost in Space*, *The Time Tunnel*, etc), producer Irwin Allen would spend the next decade earning a reputation as the "Master of Disaster", with such classics as *The Poseidon Adventure* and *The Towering Inferno*. The 1970s disaster craze was big-scale escapism, with some entries, such as *The Poseidon Adventure*, the jewel in the genre's crown.

Aboard a luxury liner on the way from New York to Athens, the merry passengers of the *SS Poseidon* get their ship turned over by a massive tidal wave, and a handful of survivors, led by a rebellious priest (Gene Hackman), must now leave the sinking ship.

Essentially, *The Poseidon Adventure* isn't just an old disaster flick our dads watched; it's a tale of survival and human courage. Behind the impressive special effects is the theme echoed by Hackman's renegade reverend – that people should fight for others and not pray to God to save themselves.

Hackman's Reverend Scott, fiery and single-minded in his belief that the survivors can overcome their ordeal, encourages survivors to climb to the bottom of the overturned ship, urging Belle (Shelley Winters) that, "life is up there. And life always matters".

Hackman's Reverend Scott is an excellent role model, stirring the human spirit so that *SS Poseidon*'s washed-up survivors can gain the desire and will to survive. Along with a few Oscars, *The Poseidon Adventure* would earn a belated sequel, *Beyond the Poseidon Adventure*, where footage from the original film would be recycled, as a bored Telly Savalas pondered where his career had gone. Directed by Ronald Neame and produced by disaster specialist Irwin Allen, *The Poseidon Adventure* is a story of courage, sacrifice and human endeavour.

"Everyone's looking for a way to escape"

On many occasions, the brand of family entertainment furnished by Steven Spielberg over many generations gets mentioned by young people. It may be something from their parent's age group, like *E.T. the Extra-Terrestrial* or *Jurassic Park* or something a bit more modern like *The Adventures of Tintin*. A few years ago, one such film was recommended to me.

Steven Spielberg's *Ready Player One* is set in 2045 and is based on Ernest Cline's novel. The film takes us on a 1980s nostalgia trip and lives up to the hype spun by many enthusiastic young people. The story of *Ready Player One* centres on an orphaned teenager who escapes reality by entering the virtual world of the "Oasis".

The CGI-packed narrative follows orphaned teenager Wade Watts (Tye Sheridan), who lives with his aunt in a rundown area of Columbus, Ohio. Most of society spends more than half their day strapping on VR technology whilst entering the immersive world of the Oasis, where you can be whoever you wish to be and choose how you look with a nifty avatar.

Echoing *Willy Wonka and the Chocolate Factory*, playful genius and co-creator of the Oasis, James Halliday (Mark Rylance) tells the world that anyone competing in a series of puzzles will win possession of the Oasis.

Behind the guise of an avatar called Parzival, Wade bands together a group of willing young heroes and sets out on his quest. Only corporate bad guy Noah Sorrento (Ben Mendelsohn) stands in his way as he wants to take control of the Oasis for his own financial gain.

The narrative switches from the real world of Wade's impoverished junk yard caravan park and the virtual world of the Oasis – "a place where the limits of reality are your own imagination". This theme of living in the real world rang a bell with young people, as one young person stated, "As most of my mates play games on our phones or make videos on TikTok, this makes more sense to me than someone old." That was me told.

As a lead character and role model, Wade reveals excellent leadership skills and integrity as he finds friendship and love with Samantha (Olivia Cooke). In James Halliday, Wade sees a shade of his future self and realises the importance of living his life in the real world, not necessarily in a virtual one.

Crammed with pop culture references, *Ready Player One* offers viewers a nostalgic road trip and big-budget sci-fi. Along the way, there's the DeLorean from *Back to the Future*, Chucky from *Child's Play* and the clever use of the Overlook Hotel from *The Shining*. Towards the end of *Ready Player One*, Wade makes a passionate speech inspiring people to come with him and join him, as he has now found friendship and love. An excellent cinematic role model.

"Just think what you can do for the world"

Based on the rebooted game from 2013, a new *Tomb Raider* film allows Lara Croft another crack at the box office. In the late 1990s, the list of potential candidates who could fill Lara's hot pants was a mile long. There were two films with Angelina Jolie in the lead, performing well at the box office, with much of the cultural discourse concentrating on the "look" of the character.

The filmmakers rightly wanted to prove that this new version of Lara Croft differed from the boob-obsessed Angelina Jolie additions from the turn of the century. Swedish actress Alicia Vikander is a more contemporary, trendy Lara Croft with a washboard stomach and severe Daddy issues.

In this new film, Lara's father is missing and presumed dead. When Lara finds a handy pre-recorded video message from her dad (Dominic West), informing her about a fabled Japanese tomb, Lara travels across the globe on a dangerous adventure to her dad's last-known destination.

Once you strip away the impressive action and the *Last Crusade* story arc, at its heart, *Tomb Raider* is a family drama dealing with abandonment and, before long, forgiveness and reconnection.

Perfectly performed by Alicia Vikander, this cinematic version of Lara 2.0 is a stubborn, independent, clever young woman who relies on her raw determination and family devotion. Lara is an heiress to countless millions, but the filmmakers make her more relatable and likeable by making her a skint bike courier. Alicia Vikander offers a believable performance, and her relationship with her adventurer dad, retold in a series of short flashbacks, is heartfelt.

Indeed, toning down the sexuality of Lara Croft and letting a bit more heart creep in allows this newly rebooted Lara to have a bit more insecurity.

The chase sequences and Lara's skill and habit of leaping into the air are all awe-inspiring, but the mixture of escapism and determination for Lara to reach her goal is the real winner.

> "Ladies and gentlemen, I think you'll agree with me that we have three charming children here who are indeed an example to us all"

Based on the novel by Edith Nesbit, this family favourite from director Lionel Jeffries is a mainstay of the Christmas holidays, rightfully enjoying its place as a classic of British cinema. *The Railway Children* captures the innocence of childhood and the joy of youth. It's an irresistibly charming and wholesome film.

The cosy bubble of a middle-class family bursts wide open when Charles Waterbury (Iain Cuthbertson), a kind, hard-working civil servant, is falsely arrested for selling state secrets and sent to prison. His three children, Roberta (Jenny Agutter), Phyllis (Sally Thomsett) and Peter (Gary Warren), and their devoted mother (Dinah Sheridan), move to a small house in Yorkshire called the Three Chimneys. To make ends meet, the children's mother writes and sells short stories to magazines and newspapers as the children befriend Mr Perks (Bernard Cribbins), the station porter of the local train station, and a kindly old gentleman (William Mervyn).

Best exemplified during the scene of Roberta's birthday, where she seems to float around the room accepting birthday presents, *The Railway Children* depicts a dreamy world of gentle nostalgia and childhood playfulness. Due to the story's episodic nature, we see the children in different modes; we witness their virtues and qualifications as good role models: the children's courage in stopping the train after a landslide, their kindness in helping the Russian writer find his family and their friendship with Mr Perks on his birthday.

Did this world of kind strangers and wholesome loveable characters ever exist? Who cares, as it exists in *The Railway Children*, and that's why each new generation falls for its charms with each further seasonal viewing. *The Railway Children* is effortlessly sweet, with the sequence of the children's father emerging from the steam on the railway platform unforgettable – an enchanting film for all ages.

"Down here it's our time. It's our time, down here!"

Anyone alive in the 1980s has seen *The Goonies*, that self-named rag-tag group of adolescents who discover an old map and embark on a quest to find hidden treasure.

In order to save their neighbourhood from unscrupulous land developers, young Mikey leads the Goonies on a daring adventure to find the fortune of One-Eyed Willy, a mysterious old pirate from the seventeenth century. The group of young misfits that make up the Goonies are Ke Huy Quan (fresh from *Indiana Jones and the Temple of Doom*) as gadget-obsessed Data, Corey Feldman, plucked from another Spielberg production (*Gremlins*) as Mouth, with Jeff Cohen as ice-cream-loving Chunk, and Sean Astin as Mikey. In addition to the main Goonies, after displaying a talent for improvisation, future Hollywood star Josh Brolin impressed director Richard Donner during the audition stage and landed the role of Mikey's older brother Brand.

Mikey is the leader of this little gang of misfits. His

motivational speech at the bottom of a wishing well, urging his fellow Goonies to continue in their quest, is one of the pivotal sequences in the film. As it's not just the quest for One-Eyed Willy's treasure; it's the extension of their friendship, the Goonies' childhood.

Originally titled *The Goon Kids*, *The Goonies* is old-fashioned and deliberately designed that way, with nods to Errol Flynn and Tom Sawyer. *The Goonies* is about that last summer of childhood and the sense of adventure everyone carries with them.

The meaning of childhood friendship visible on the screen was not only down to Richard Donner's assured direction. The production team also rented a hotel for a month, where the cast and crew could live together, living and working as one big family – what remains onscreen is the joy of unchecked youthfulness, where the young cast spends much of their time screaming and laughing.

A cherished and beloved film for most people who grew up in the 1980s, *The Goonies* has everything; an exciting adventure, likeable characters, straightforward plotting, clumsy crooks (Robert Davi and Joe Pantoliano) and child-friendly scares. Based on a story by Steven Spielberg, *The Goonies* has remained as popular as ever, as friends search for one last adventure, sharing friendship and excitement.

"More connects us than separates us"

There is sometimes a celebration evening at the end of a youth work project. Typically, this occurs at the cinema, with the usual accompaniment of popcorn, soft drinks and plenty of overexcitement. In hindsight, *Black Panther* seemed like the "water cooler moment" of 2018; this was the Marvel film to see that year.

Black Panther is a superhero film that considers representation, colonisation, empowerment and how to kick ass. Ryan Coogler, who, with the 2015 release of *Creed*, breathed fresh air into the *Rocky* series, pulls together one of the best Marvel films, which, as well as considering oppression, gender equality and identity, is a stylish, afro-futuristic, action-packed superhero film.

First introduced in Marvel's *Captain America: Civil War*, the late Chadwick Boseman plays T'Challa, and, after the death of his father, takes the throne of the fictional land of Wakanda, becoming Wakanda's new king. T'Challa battles with the vengeful Shakespearean villain Erik Killmonger (Michael B. Jordan), who believes he has the "blood right" to be king of Wakanda – a country which appears to the outside world as a third world country but is a technologically advanced society.

After watching *Black Panther*, during the post-cinema discussion, everyone seemed to find the main character, all suited up in a high-tech, sleek *Iron Man*-styled suit, as the cool new hero in mainstream cinema. I enjoyed the welcome dash of James Bond thrown into the mix as T'Challa visits casinos and stops by his sixteen-year-old sister Shuri's (Letitia Wright) Q-styled lab, displaying all the modern gadgetry and cool suits.

Although some of the CGI looks a bit naff, the action set pieces, particularly the sequence at the casino, are very well executed, with flashy cinematography by Rachel Morrison.

Now there is a significant superhero character who is non-white, reassuring the belief that we can all be superheroes regardless of colour, gender or background. Gone are the well-worn wisecracks of Tony Stark; presented here is a more soulful approach to heroism. As a role model, T'Challa/Black Panther is a charismatic leader, brave and ultra-cool.

There are also the women of Wakanda to consider, with Angela Bassett as the wise matriarch, Queen Ramonda, tech genius Shuri and Wakandan warrior General Okoye (Danai Gurira). These women are not merely set dressing; they are vital to the success of Black Panther's conflict with Erik Killmonger.

Director Richard Donner suggested many years ago, "You'll believe a man can fly." In *Black Panther*, forty years on from Donner's *Superman*, you can believe that anyone can be a superhero, regardless of background, class or ethnicity – a fantastic role model.

"I believe in you"

Whistle Down the Wind is an enchanting children's movie where a trio of siblings befriend a criminal, mistaking the crook for Jesus Christ. Based on the novel by Mary Hayley Bell, her daughter Hayley Mills leads the youthful cast in this whimsical tale of childhood innocence.

Produced in the early 1960s, three young siblings, Kathy (Hayley Mills), Charles (Alan Barnes) and Nan (Diane Holgate), rescue some kittens from drowning in a nearby stream, hiding the kittens in a farmyard barn. Later, the eldest sibling, Kathy, finds a man hiding in the barn and mistakes the man for Jesus Christ. The children nurse their mysterious stranger back to health, stocking up on toothpaste, soap and a fruit pie.

There are a couple of scenes where adults share the screen to explain a bit of the plot. Yet, most of the narrative is told from the children's point of view – their innocence and self-imposed duty to protect the Second Coming of Jesus Christ.

News of the return of Jesus spreads among other children from around the area, with a dozen children becoming his disciples and forming "a secret society from the grown-ups". However, the man hiding in the barn is not Jesus, but a criminal, wanted for murder and hiding from the police.

It's a beautifully produced children's film brought to the screen by British cinema titans Richard Attenborough and Bryan Forbes. Told through children's eyes, *Whistle Down the Wind* depicts the children's values, moral compass and worldview. Arthur Ibbetson's crisp black-and-white cinematography and delightful performances from a young cast only add to the cosiness and warmth of a tale that could have easily veered into nauseating sentimentality.

Whistle Down the Wind is one of the best children's films ever made. Seeing the world from the children's eyes, we see the children's distinct view of their world, their social ecology and their generosity and empathy towards a stranger found in a barn.

Throughout this playful tale of childhood, there is an intentional parallel to the story of Christ; the playground denial of Christ with a train whistle replacing the rooster crow and even a spirited rendition of 'We Three Kings' weaved throughout Malcolm Arnold's charming soundtrack – overall a great film.

"When given the choice between being right or being kind, choose kind"

During a group work session where young people planned an anti-bullying film, the conversation jumped from the documentary styled *A Girl Like Her* to more comedic fare like *Drillbit Taylor*. Clive Owens' 2011 drama *Trust* got some airtime as the group discussed the film's narrative of a teenage girl meeting a boyfriend online who turns out to be a man pushing forty.

The film that got the most attention was *Wonder*, starring Owen Wilson and Julia Roberts as parents to a small boy trying to find his place in life as he begins school. August "Auggie" Pullman (Jacob Tremblay), has had many facial surgeries due to a rare medical condition and, having been home-schooled by his mother, is starting school as a fifth grader.

In *Wonder*, there are the standard tropes of Auggie finding his share of bullies and his journey of finding supportive teachers and friends, but the film steers clear of ever becoming too sappy. Based on the novel of the same name by R. J. Palacio, *Wonder* is as much about acceptance and compassion as it is about bullying and ignorance. We get other characters' perspectives through various narrative viewpoints, which offer insight into their lives and that "everyone is fighting a hard battle".

It's the TikTok generation version of *The Elephant Man*,

examining the theme of man's inhumanity to man while also revealing that with decent values and humanity, we are all on life's long road together. The film examines social inclusion and the importance that everyone, regardless of ability, skin colour, socioeconomic background or religious beliefs, deserves their place to get the most out of life.

Wonder spoke to me as someone who grew up feeling different due to challenges with my speech and now having a twelve-year-old son with special educational needs. Although that's just it, the film speaks to everyone. Feeling loved and accepted is a collective human experience, particularly when young. *Wonder* is about opening your eyes wider and seeing that everyone is equal and deserving of kindness, compassion and friendship.

"If we run now, we lose more than a game"

One of the most absurd yet best-ever escapist films produced about the Second World War mixes actors who can't play football and footballers who can't act. A cult favourite, usually propping up the television schedules when a World Cup comes around, *Escape to Victory* is a silly wartime caper involving Allied POWs taking on the German national team in a football match in France.

A plump Michael Caine plays West Ham and England footballer John Colby, who coaches a team of international favourites, including Pelé, Osvaldo Ardiles, Bobby Moore and Paul Van Himst. The Germans view the match as a tool for mass propaganda, yet the prisoners of war, particularly the Allied officers, view the match as the perfect opportunity to escape.

Based on actual events, *Escape to Victory* ignores the historical accuracy and combines *The Great Escape* with England's fascination with football, resulting in a stirring Second World War drama.

The footballing sequences or "plays" designed by Pelé are visually striking, with slick dribbling, crunching tackles and sublime overhead kicks. Director John Huston splices much of the training and pre-match discussions with an exciting escape plot with American import Sylvester Stallone as escapee-cum-goalie Hatch.

Yet, Stallone is probably given too much screen time, including a boring love story involving French Resistance sweetheart Renée (Carole Laure). The tense and dramatic football sequence during the finale is much more successful, expertly filmed and enhanced with Bill Conti's spirited score.

Escape to Victory is arguably the best film ever produced about the beautiful game. Luckily, Pelé, Bobby Moore and the rest of the team don't have much acting to do and save their talents for the football pitch, leaving Michael Caine and Max von Sydow (as a football-mad German major) to do much of the heavy lifting.

As a young child watching the film, I found the film inspiring – the players' determination to continue and never give up when the odds are against them. It's the go-to film for anyone who likes football but who is not necessarily a film fan. It's the textbook combination of old cinema tropes and sporting giants – perfect for a sleepy Sunday afternoon.

> "Losing family obliges us to find our family. Not always the family that is our blood, but the family that can become our blood"

After a late-career resurgence with *The Rock* in 1996, Sean Connery moved away from the action fare that made him a star and played a crusty old writer who begins a unique friendship with a confident and gifted young man.

In *Finding Forrester*, Connery is William Forrester, a reclusive Pulitzer Prize-winning novelist who spends much of his time peeping out the window at his neighbourhood below.

Curiosity gets the better of some of the neighbourhood kids as Jamal (Rob Brown in his debut role) gets swayed by his buddies into sneaking into Forrester's upper-floor apartment. Forrester soon catches Jamal creeping about his flat, scaring him. Nevertheless, a strange and intriguing friendship soon follows.

The Name of the Rose, *Highlander* and a few other films within his back catalogue cast Connery as the older, wiser mentor with a younger protégé. In *Finding Forrester*, Connery is no different, as the older William Forrester encourages the writer within Jamal to "punch the keys" and become the best version of himself.

Jamal feels the pressure of proving himself academically in the classroom and athletically on the basketball court. Due to his basketball skills and brilliant test scores, Jamal gets a scholarship to a high-end school. As a bright black kid from the Bronx hiding in plain sight on a basketball court, Jamal is pressured into hiding his intelligence and literary talents and finds life difficult.

Just as Jamal and Forrester's friendship deepens, a pompous English teacher (F. Murray Abraham) pigeonholes Jamal as nothing more academic than a basketball player, accusing him of plagiarism.

Pressured into winning a basketball match for the school, Jamal finds his moment to take ownership of his destiny. Throughout *Finding Forrester* runs the theme of friendship and the clash of cultures. There's also the importance of not pigeonholing young people and not pressuring people to win basketball tournaments or gain high grades at school. Perhaps more suited for the more mature young person, *Finding Forrester* finds Sean Connery, in his penultimate screen role, perfectly cast as Forrester. His friendship with Jamal is funny, insightful and heartfelt – a lesson in friendship, hope, and integrity.

"If you ever need me, I'll be there for you, in your thoughts and in your dreams"

Fast-forward to 2015 and an alternative to the *Harry Potter* series, suggested by one young person, got the group talking. *Percy Jackson and the Lightning Thief* sounded like the remake of *Clash of the Titans*, only with kids and a better script. A special educational needs coordinator had placed this young person on a waiting list for an ASD (autism spectrum disorder) assessment. Their parents suggested *Little Man Tate*, the early '90s film about a child prodigy, and the thought-provoking 2011 film *Extremely Loud & Incredibly Close*, where a young autistic child tries to make sense of a world without his father.

After many conversations, I thought this young person may not want to see a film that "was about" behavioural challenges – just a film connected to behavioural challenges. In *Percy Jackson*, Percy (Logan Lerman) is a teenage boy who discovers he's the son of the Greek god Poseidon. Percy has dyslexia and ADHD and feels isolated. He believes he's a loser but feels at home in the water, showing a fantastic ability to stay underwater for long periods.

Struggling at school, Percy lives with his mother and abusive stepfather, Gabe (Joe Pantoliano). Due to his stepdad smelling "like a sewer" and sleeping to noon, Percy has no active male role model in daily life but routinely stands up to his stepdad's abusive behaviour.

Percy learns his true heritage at Camp Half-Blood, a training camp for demi-gods. Percy hones his fighting skills at the base and discovers that his dyslexia and ADHD are his "greatest gifts". His brain is hardwired to ancient Greek so that he can unravel ancient Greek phrases, and his ADHD and impulsive behaviour means he's battle ready.

With Grover (Brandon T. Jackson), Percy's junior protector, and Annabeth (Alexandra Daddario), his sword-swinging love interest, Percy begins an adventure to prevent a war between the Greek gods, whilst also rescuing his kidnapped mother (Catherine Keener) from the evil clutches of Hades, played by Steve Coogan.

Although it deviates from the bestselling book by Rick Riordan, *Percy Jackson and the Lightning Thief* is an enjoyable film. There was a sequel in 2013, *Percy Jackson: Sea of Monsters*, before the series migrated to the small screen on Disney+. Director Chris Columbus had spearheaded the first two *Harry Potter* films, and the producers probably hoped with *Percy* that lightning would strike twice with this franchise. Although not the mammoth box office hit that *Harry Potter* was, *Percy Jackson* still has enough action and spectacle to please most Potter fans.

In conversation with that particular young person, it was clear that they connected with the story and the character of Percy Jackson, and who could blame them? Overall, Percy displays excellent leadership skills as a lead character. He leads his small team of adventurers with his instincts and a more extraordinary ability to believe in himself as he finally accepts who he is.

"They can be a great people, Kal-El, they wish to be. They only lack the light to show the way. For this reason, above all, their capacity for good, I have sent them you... my only son"

The grandaddy and originator of big-screen superhero movies, *Superman: The Movie*, to give its full title, is the gold standard of superhero films. Director Richard Donner creates a fantasy world of truth and justice in a post-Watergate era of American society.

Superman is a tongue-in-cheek adventure that stands the test of time, combining excellent special effects and a beautiful score by John Williams. Robert Redford, Warren Beatty and Nick Nolte were all played around as potential Supermen before actor Christopher Reeve got the nod, setting the bar for anyone else who would ever play the Man of Steel.

The film begins on Superman's home planet, where we meet Superman's dad Jor-El, played by Marlon Brando, an expensive addition to the cast but well worth it, as Brando adds a lot of gravitas to a deliberately biblical and grandiose opening sequence.

Just before Krypton, Superman's home planet, explodes in outer space, Jor-El sends his baby son Kal-El to Earth.

Living on a farm in Smallville, baby Kal-El becomes Clark Kent, gains another kind father in Jonathan Kent (Glenn Ford) and begins his new life on Earth.

The final section of the film is a pure comic book adventure as Clark arrives at the *Daily Planet* in Metropolis and meets street-smart reporter Lois Lane (Margot Kidder) and criminal genius Lex Luthor (Gene Hackman). There are missiles, earthquakes, great dialogue and massive action set pieces. It's one of the best superhero films ever made.

As Superman flies around saving the world and falling in love with Lois Lane, the film also celebrates difference. Superman is the quintessential outsider. He feels different from every other person on Earth. Growing up on a farm in Smallville, Clark had to try and fit in with the other kids at school. As an adult in Metropolis, he had to try to fit into his new life as a reporter, adopting a new persona as an endearing clown in the *Daily Planet* newsroom.

As a cinematic role model, it's hard to beat Superman. Sure, he has X-ray vision, flies, is super strong and so on. But his real power is his humanity; he sees the good in people. He is also faithful to himself and the best version of himself.

As viewers, we have X-ray vision, as we can see right through him; Superman is the purest and most straightforward superhero. He is goodness personified – a super role model.

"No one ever made a difference by being like everyone else"

A box office phenomenon on its initial release, *The Greatest Showman* is a bona fide family classic. Based on the story of American showman P. T. Barnum, played by *X-Men* star Hugh Jackman, *The Greatest Showman* tells the tale of the Barnum & Bailey Circus through catchy songs, showstopping dance routines and soul-searching melodrama.

Young people flocked to the cinema in their droves to see the film when *The Greatest Showman* was first released in 2017. The fresh shiny faces of Zac Efron and Zendaya and the film's many memorable tunes probably got young people through the door, but the celebration of diversity kept them in the cinema. The film spoke to their generation. A film that embraces difference and promotes acceptance.

American songwriting duo Benj Pasek and Justin Paul, who had composed the songs for the musical *La La Land*, came up trumps again in *The Greatest Showman*, loaded with many memorable songs. One in particular, the floor filler 'This Is Me', conveys the narrative's core themes of inclusivity and individualism. In the story, the bearded lady, Lettie Lutz (Keala Settle), shunned by Barnum at a party, belts out 'This Is Me', revealing pride, vulnerability, power and strength. A song about self-love, not hiding who you are, accepting yourself and being brave – the perfect message for young people.

When I did see the film, I could understand why it was such a monster hit. I knew of the Jim Dale Broadway musical *Barnum* from the 1980s, but I slowly became aware of the rapid word of mouth and infectious joy that *The Greatest Showman* was spreading: the choreography, the songs, the vast spectacle – a sure classic for generations to come.

A mix of colour and imagination

Released forty years before I was born, *Fantasia* has plenty to offer most audiences. As an adult, I appreciate the artistry of *Fantasia*, its experimentation and bravery. As a child, however, I enjoyed the explosion of colour and the sound of Tchaikovsky's 'Dance of the Sugar Plum Fairy'.

In 1940, Disney's *Fantasia* offered audiences a tour-de-force of extraordinary animation juxtaposed with classical music. Following the success of *Snow White and the Seven Dwarfs* and *Pinocchio*, *Fantasia* is a bold experiment, beautifully crafted on a lavish scale.

Music critic and composer Deems Taylor is the Master of ceremonies, standing among an orchestra of musicians, featuring English composer Leopold Stokowski and the Philadelphia Orchestra. Taylor introduces us to *Fantasia*, often popping up to introduce each segment.

We move between each musical composition, accompanied by stunning animation (some of these sequences may scare sensitive viewers) depicting ancient mythology, dinosaurs, beautiful fairies and who else but

Mickey Mouse in the film's most famous segment, 'The Sorcerer's Apprentice'.

As a young boy apprehensive about learning yet another phrase or the right way to pronounce a word, *Fantasia* was perfect. It offered no role model to latch on to but took me on a fascinating journey of imagination, an early beginning in cinema therapy – just the simple practice of immersing myself in rich storytelling, bold colours and relaxing music.

Fantasia is a visual feast full of bold colours and bursts of light, introducing children to soothing classical music, which worked wonderfully well with the stunning animations. Some older children may find the movie boring, although *Fantasia* is perfect for anyone who appreciates traditional animation.

"In the name of God, do your duty"

The horror of real life can often make anyone turn to the silver screen or the tiny screen of a mobile device, anything for a distraction. It could be the cost of living, a war in a far-off country or the general feeling of life getting you down.

International events can shake the world, such as the grotesque and unwarranted murder of George Floyd by a white police officer in May 2020, which sparked worldwide protests against racial discrimination and police brutality.

George Floyd's brutal murder led to global discussion, raising the profile of the Black Lives Matter movement. The discussion I shared with a group on racial prejudice was a microcosm of what was happening worldwide in classrooms and community centres. George Floyd's brutal murder was a moment to pause and collectively view our compassion for others.

During the session, I suggested looking at the film *To Kill a Mockingbird*, which examines racial bigotry and small-town ignorance in 1930s Alabama. In his finest role, Gregory Peck plays Atticus Finch, a southern lawyer who defends Tom Robinson (Brock Peters), a black man accused of raping a white girl. Widowed, living on a dirt road in a small house in the fictional town of Maycomb, Atticus Finch is also father to tomboy daughter Scout (Mary Badham) and her older brother Jem (Phillip Alford).

To Kill a Mockingbird centres on the children's loss of innocence and, in the case of their scary neighbour Boo Radley (Robert Duvall), a lesson on being less judgemental of another individual. Much of the narrative focuses on their innocent view of the world, their fear of a supposedly scary neighbour and their friendship with Dill (John Megna), a visiting neighbour.

An intense courtroom segment takes up the better part of the film's second half. On trial for rape, as Atticus Finch fights for justice and human decency, his client, Tom Robinson, is innocent of wrongdoing, as the film shines a light on prejudice and racial injustice.

Hollywood legend Gregory Peck was born to play Atticus Finch. With it, Peck offers up one of cinema's most positive and admirable role models, finding the number one spot in the American Film Institute's list of the hundred greatest heroes in cinema.

Produced in the early 1960s, before the Vietnam War's intensity and Martin Luther King Jr's assassination, *To Kill a Mockingbird* can provoke engaging discussion on racial politics, bigotry and the civil rights movement. Adapted from the Pulitzer Prize-winning novel by Harper Lee, *To Kill a Mockingbird* is an important film and an even greater lesson in humanity.

"Each man's life touches so many other lives"

The discussion with young people began with the 2008 film *Ghost Town*, a comedy starring Ricky Gervais, where a grumpy dentist can see dead people. Some of the discussion went straight to the '90s thriller *The Game* – a film packed with profanity, with scenes depicting suicide and one scene in particular of a sexual nature.

Although aimed towards adults, aided with a heavy dose of Hitchcock and with a twist on *A Christmas Carol*, *The Game* sees Michael Douglas's Scrooge-like Nicholas Van Orton finding redemption and the slow realisation that relationships and people are more important than money and possessions. There was further discussion on the 1990s classic *Groundhog Day*, where a self-absorbed weatherman (Bill Murray) relives the same day countless times, learning life lessons throughout the running time.

All the individuals at the community centre were young and unemployed, wondering if life had left them behind. Growing up, passing through life and maturing through adolescence is complicated, with that day's conversation drifting towards films with themes of redemption, unfulfilled dreams, regrets and ambitions.

Sometimes we can lose sight of the need to remember our self-worth. We listen with too much intent to our inner critic, that voice inside doubting our beliefs, knocking our achievements and flatlining our hope for the future. Listening to that voice too much will affect your self-esteem, confidence and mental health. You could mentally block that voice in your head or, better still, talk to a friend or a medical professional. You could re-examine your inner critic's evidence, see how accurate it is, or – do what I do – and watch an uplifting film.

After everyone aired their opinions on everything from *The Game* to *Groundhog Day*, I pointed to a famous uplifting movie, George Bailey's (James Stewart) story in *It's a Wonderful Life*. A post-war classic where a man realises his self-value. A film that the American Film Institute proudly placed as number one on their list of the most inspiring movies of all time – a timeless tale of a decent man realising that every "life touches so many other lives".

Offering a funny, engaging and dramatic slice of Americana, we watch George grow up as a young boy, through the 1920s and into the war years. George never leaves his hometown of Bedford Falls, never explores the world and believes his life is a failure and that the world would be better without him.

In a pit of despair and contemplating suicide, George is offered a chance to see the world without him by a guardian angel (Henry Travers). The angel presents George with another timeline, one where George wasn't there to help people, change their lives or make a difference.

The film examines the importance of valuing your existence, regardless of when life gets in the way of your best-laid plans.

It's a Wonderful Life was not an initial success, only

becoming a family favourite due to repeated broadcasts on television. Rich in heart and memorable in its conviction that "no man is a failure", *It's a Wonderful Life* is a truly wonderful film.

"It does not do to dwell on dreams and forget to live"

First published in the 1990s, J. K. Rowling's *Harry Potter and the Philosopher's Stone* was a colossal hit. Naturally, a film franchise would follow when the Potter books sold well into the millions. Movie studio Warner Bros selected Steven Spielberg's protégée Chris Columbus to bring Harry Potter to the big screen; with the screenplay staying faithful to the novel, the filmmakers created a memorable supernatural adventure and an influential film franchise.

Harry Potter is an orphan; his parents murdered, and he lives with his cruel uncle and auntie, who have little time or love for Harry. On his eleventh birthday, Harry learns he's a wizard and heads off to Hogwarts, a boarding school for wizards.

Accompanied by a fanfare of trumpets on John Williams' majestic score, we follow Harry's introduction to Hogwarts with his new friends, Ron Weasley (Rupert Grint) and Hermione Granger (Emma Watson), as he meets new foes such as Eminem-lookalike Draco Malfoy (Tom Felton). Stuck between two boys, Hermione is bright and determined, and Ron Weasley is funny and brave – and probably made having gingery-red hair fashionable.

Picking out the best *Harry Potter* film is a bit like

asking who the best James Bond is, but for what it's worth, unlike later entries in the series, this first film is more light-hearted, with just enough scares, like the memorable scene with the enormous troll.

Armed with a massive budget and impressive special effects, the filmmakers recreate the book's magical world. But behind all the spectacle is the central character of Harry Potter, who is intelligent, heroic and resourceful. He's a brave role model for an entire generation, rising above his unfortunate beginning in life and the terrible role models he had growing up.

"All I wanna do is go the distance"

One film from the 1970s always gets mentioned when I'm discussing powerful cinematic role models. If you have never seen *Rocky*, the boxing drama about a small-time boxer who gets his chance in the ring with a heavyweight champion, you have at least heard of it.

It's a cultural landmark in popular culture, beat *Taxi Driver* to an Oscar and made a star out of Sylvester Stallone. I have no interest in boxing, but *Rocky* contains the basic story of human resilience, the human spirit and the importance of believing in yourself.

When champion boxer Apollo Creed (Carl Weathers) needs a new boxing opponent when his scheduled fighter gets injured, Apollo selects a local boxer called Rocky Balboa as his new opponent. Rocky works as an enforcer for a local loan shark living in a rough area in Philadelphia. He gets trained by Mickey Goldmill (a crusty Burgess Meredith) while falling in love with

Adrian (Talia Shire), a shy pet shop worker. Rocky may want to go the distance with Apollo in the ring and find his self-respect, but even more so, Rocky wishes to win Adrian's heart.

In the finale, Apollo and Rocky slug it out in the ring, aided by James Crabes incredible use of low cross-angle camera compositions. Yet, the real winner is Adrian's relationship with Rocky; their awkward, wholesome romance is at the heart of *Rocky*.

The story of Rocky's journey to overcome his insecurities and realise his potential mirrors Sylvester Stallone's journey of getting the film on the big screen. After a half dozen bit parts in films with Woody Allen, Jack Lemmon and Robert Mitchum, Stallone reportedly wrote the script for *Rocky* in three days.

His script got studio attention, but the deal was always for another actor to get the gloves on. Yet Stallone held firm, landed the part of Rocky and changed the course of his career. His performance in the film was nominated for an Oscar, and his performance drew comparisons to a young Marlon Brando.

There are, of course, the *Rocky* sequels; some are better than others. The cheesiest sequel is *Rocky IV*, where Rocky tries to sort out the Cold War by banging heads with Dolph Lundgren, and *Rocky V*, which is so bad, it just begs the question, *Why?* Barring *Rocky Balboa*, none of the other sequels can pull at the heartstrings like the original *Rocky* film. The franchise became so mercilessly recycled in parodies and advertisements that it became dumb.

Filmed on location, *Rocky* has grit and heart; his character is likeable, and his romance with Adrian is believable.

And believe is the keyword in *Rocky* – a sports drama nonetheless, but one that can make you believe in yourself.

Move over, Jimmy?

After much fanfare and equal tabloid dismay and pre-judgement, Pierce Brosnan's uber-cool Bond made way for Daniel Craig's tough and buffed Bond with the franchise rebooting with 2006's *Casino Royale*.

The series did away with the "one and done" films of the earlier series and created a narrative string of five films, with *Skyfall* being the best of the five. Although Daniel Craig has many fans in action-adventure cinema, the *Mission Impossible* and *Fast & Furious* franchises have superseded the Bond series as the top action series in mainstream cinema.

Everyone talked about the newest stunt in a *Mission Impossible* film. "The stunts are amazing," said one young person, a thirteen-year-old who rarely visited the cinema. They were going through a tough time at school and found the cinema experience of watching Tom Cruise jump around buildings exhilarating. They enjoyed the escapism, the fantasy, the spectacle.

The *Mission Impossible* film series is America's answer to James Bond. With Lalo Schifrin's timeless theme tune and international espionage blended with big-budget action, the *Mission Impossible* series is the escape for many young people today that I found with James Bond films at school.

Created by Bruce Geller, the *Mission Impossible* television series of the 1960s, '70s and 1980s (if you include the dire Australian update) chronicled the adventures of a small team of government agents who, with a mixture of teamwork, clever disguises and sophisticated methods of deception, outwitted war criminals and foreign dictators.

With its ingenious plotting and jazzy music score, the original television series ran from 1966 to 1973 and is top-drawer escapism. The minimal use of dialogue and the emphasis on teamwork drew me towards the series – it's just great entertainment with a great ensemble cast.

Master filmmaker Brian De Palma kickstarted the Tom Cruise film series in 1996. The original series cast was hopeful of being included in this new film, but their hope turned to outrage as they realised that team leader Jim Phelps would become a bad guy in the Cruise film.

The *Mission Impossible* film series continues, with each entry pushing the action dial further up, as the series' identity moves further away from the origins of the television show. Cruise's Ethan Hunt isn't the sensible silver-haired leader of Jim Phelps from the television series. He's Bond, with an American accent and, judging by what I have learned from young people, is a modern cinematic role model – in a film series where you can park your brain, sit back and escape life.

In terms of Vin Diesel and co – packed with illegal street races and cheesy dialogue scenes on the bonnet of a Dodge Charger, the *Fast & Furious* franchise began with turbo-charged driving sequences, before morphing into a full-blown film franchise with preposterous action set pieces – the characters transforming from adrenalin-fuelled street racers to indestructible beefcakes taking on cyber terrorists and international bad guys.

As the *Fast & Furious* franchise continues with even more sequels, the storylines have become even more convoluted. Although some young people, during a group chat on Zoom, thought the action set pieces in the *Furious* films were "immense" and that I was missing the point. They didn't watch for the storylines; they watched the *Furious* movies to "relax from a hard day at school". Yet, during the same conversation, one seventeen-year-old, who had enjoyed the films since they were four, believed that the *Furious* movies were stupid for anyone over ten years old, as the characters spend half the running time banging on about "family", only to spend the rest of the film doing nothing but driving cars and blowing stuff up.

At any rate, everyone agreed that the *Fast & Furious* franchise was still in first gear concerning interesting female characters. Everyone pointed towards the *Star Wars* saga, with Rey, Leia and Padmé Amidala, as a film series with better female role models.

Even the *Pirates of the Caribbean* films featuring Keira Knightley as Elizabeth Swann got more recognition – a female character that many in our discussion rated as an excellent female role model, a fierce heroine in a world of crusty male pirates. When discussing action and adventure heroines, young people remarked how inspiring Knightley's character was as a young heroine who was flawed but brave, and, most importantly, more than just mere set decoration like many female characters in the *Fast & Furious* franchise.

Some young people in the group suggested that, compared with the sexualisation of female characters in the *Fast & Furious* franchise, Knightley's Elizabeth Swann was much more acceptable and likeable than the central female role of Letty Ortiz (Michelle Rodriguez) in the *Fast & Furious* films and less whiny than Bella Swan (Kristen Stewart) in the *Twilight* saga.

During the conversation with young people about characters in action and adventure cinema, I noted that time had perhaps caught up with James Bond films. Maybe the Bond series is unable to keep up with the pace of the *Mission Impossible* and *Fast & Furious* franchises. If so, the Bond producers may have to expand the Bond universe, create separate adventures for the other 00s, or bring Bond back to his mid-twentieth century beginnings and produce period Bond films.

Bond might have to reinvent itself and prove there is more to action cinema than Vin Diesel flipping cars and gurning at the camera. Whatever the case, with the *Fast & Furious* franchise riding high at the box office, Bond will have to re-establish itself and let young audiences know that, just like a trailer for an '80s Bond film had promised: "In the world of high adventure, the highest number is still 007."

"I was supposed to be something I didn't like"

Outland is a film everyone can relate to, particularly when discussing peer pressure and the dangers of young people following the wrong crowd.

Deliberately channelling *High Noon* from thirty years earlier, *Outland* is a slick sci-fi flick about a man with few friends trying to do the right thing when everyone around him looks the other way.

Jerry Goldsmith's eerie score sets the scene deep in outer space. There's a series of mysterious deaths on a mining colony on one of Jupiter's moons, as an honourable police marshal (Sean Connery) decides to go up against one of the head bad guys (Peter Boyle) behind a nefarious narcotics ring.

Apart from a cantankerous doctor played by Frances Sternhagen, Connery's brave marshal is isolated and alone, speaking to his family through a computer, yet he still makes the right decision. He doesn't follow convention, follow the crowd or disregard the corruption that surrounds him. Doing the right thing sets him free. He gains ownership of his beliefs, denies the bad guys and prepares to defeat them by standing his ground.

Standing up for what is right is difficult, especially when everyone around you is against you. In *Outland*, the marshal's integrity comes at a price; it alienates him and leaves him with nothing but his convictions.

Better suited for the more mature young person, *Outland* is an enjoyable thriller with some gory violence. The pace of *Outland* may be a little slow, but the story is timeless. Director Peter Hyams mixes genres, creating a splendid sci-fi thriller – a story about heroism and the belief that one person can make a difference.

"If you don't follow through on your dreams, you might as well be a vegetable"

Based on a true story, *The World's Fastest Indian* is an endearing story of human endurance, ambition and bravery in leaving your comfort zone and following your dreams. Set in the 1960s, Burt Munro is from Invercargill, a small village in New Zealand, and has spent years tinkering with his 1920 Indian motorcycle. Burt's dream is to take his bike to the Bonneville Salt Flats in Utah, where he tests himself and his bike among the best speed demons in the world.

Burt is a cheerful chap who loves life and is persistent in realising his dream. Anthony Hopkins, who had already played record-breaker Donald Campbell in an earlier television movie, is perfectly cast as Burt, bringing warmth and integrity to the role. Burt is a force of life, an underdog with self-belief and raw determination – a fish out of water, travelling halfway around the world to a different culture.

As Burt was obsessed with reaching the Bonneville Salt Flats, director Roger Donaldson was obsessed with getting his vision onscreen, spending thirty years getting the film up and running.

It's a film full of heart as it examines Burt coming to terms with his life, peeing on his lemon tree – yes, peeing on a lemon tree – and enjoying a friendship with a young boy who lives next to his workshop.

Regardless that his forty-year-old bike has the wrong tires, no safety chute and a cork from a brandy bottle on his petrol tank, Burt's determination to get his motorcycle timed on the Utah Flats brings him many friends and admirers.

Brimming with passion and perseverance, Burt is an ideal role model who never stops believing that the impossible is, in fact, possible, when you have the boldness and drive to believe in yourself. *The World's Fastest Indian* is an excellent biography film with a charming performance by Anthony Hopkins and some well-executed driving scenes. Regardless of age or circumstance, it reminds us never to give up on our dreams.

"It's our only chance. If we win, those men won't have died for nothing tonight"

A stirring theme tune by Malcolm Arnold and a rugged Kirk Douglas feature in Anthony Mann's epic wartime classic, *The Heroes of Telemark*. Set during the Second World War in Norway, in the town of Rjukan, the Allies hatch a secret plan, which involves an attack on the Norsk Hydro plant, a plant used to produce heavy water necessary for creating an atomic bomb. Based on actual events, Anthony Mann's *The Heroes of Telemark* tells the tale grandly, although it squeezes all the historical events into a two-hour-ten running time.

An intense Richard Harris plays resistance leader Knut Straud, who recruits the help of physics professor Dr Rolf Pedersen (Kirk Douglas) to help destroy the heavy water plant. Early on, there's a splendid scene en route to England on a hijacked boat, where Dr Pedersen carefully edges mines away from their freighter as Knut Straud shoots pot-shots at the floating bombs.

Once back in Norway, fifty British commandos are killed when their glider smashes into a mountain, leaving only Dr Pedersen, Knut Straud and a handful of men to complete a daring raid on the heavy water plant.

Shot on location in Norway, the film looks impressive. A few years before James Bond made it a part of his repertoire, there's a great ski chase where Dr Pedersen chases along the snow after a Norwegian traitor. There's also a bit of romance when Dr Pedersen meets his ex-wife Anna (Ulla Jacobsson), which doesn't distract too much from the action.

The Heroes of Telemark, with its picturesque backdrops, great cast and beautiful music, depicts the heroism of the Norwegian resistance. As a cinematic role model, Kirk Douglas's Dr Pedersen, at first glance, begins the film as a playboy professor, but by the end of the story he's risking his life onboard a ferry to save children, proving that anyone can change when given the opportunity. An excellent war film that stands the test of time.

"We stay close. We stick together. We get through this"

Amid a crowd of young adult dystopian fantasies, *The Maze Runner* came highly recommended as a suspenseful *Lord of the Flies*-inspired rival to the *Hunger Games* franchise.

In a compelling opening sequence, our main character, Thomas (Dylan O'Brien), wakes up in an elevator, surrounded by supplies and a caged pig. Alone and frightened, he finds himself at the centre of an enormous maze where a community of boys struggle to co-exist in a strange new world.

We meet Alby (Aml Ameen), the leader of the community, who explains that the elevator Thomas was sent up on delivers fresh supplies and a new "greenie" once a month. Surveying his new surroundings on top of a *Swiss Family Robinson*-styled treehouse, Thomas learns about the community's most important rules and is warned to "never go beyond those walls".

The guy from *Love Actually* turns up and explains that the maze changes every night and that the "runners", the fastest and strongest boys in the community, "are the only ones who really know what's out there". The slow pace of the narrative builds, just as Thomas's confidence builds, and we finally see what's behind those walls as Thomas enters the maze and meets a "Griever" – a terrifying, creepy creature.

The Maze Runner also explores responsibility, peer relationships, death and independence from a young person's viewpoint. Thomas begins the film as a scared boy and, less than halfway through, matures into a strong young leader. Most of the characters, figuratively and literally, are out of place and feel different from the rest of the world, so I can understand why this film was popular among young people.

Once in the maze, the film has some horrifying moments and nail-biting sequences. Yet, the film lacks female representation; when Teresa (Kaya Scodelario), the only girl in the maze, finally shows up, she has little to do other than share a resemblance to Kristen Stewart.

The visual effects are top-notch and the performances are solid, particularly from Dylan O'Brien as Thomas and Will Poulter as a grumpy bully. The script is exposition-heavy, but *The Maze Runner* is a surprisingly effective sci-fi shocker with some heroic and youthful role models.

"Why do we fall sir? So that we can learn to pick ourselves up"

As the DC Universe and Marvel Cinematic Universe expand to a never-ending stream of superhero films, most young people will discover a favourite superhero. Now there are some people, many in fact, who rate superhero films as an overblown toy factory with movies that are always about the same thing – some bad guy wants something, and the good guys try to stop them, but they're missing the point. This is escapist cinema, a space where you can switch off your brain and relax with an engaging and familiar storyline.

Within the superhero universe, Spider-Man if not hitting the number one spot, is one of the clear favourites among many young people. Spider-Man, or more precisely Peter Parker, is relatable – he has adolescent angst, worries about his elderly relatives and has everyday relationship problems with his teenage girlfriend. Spider-Man doesn't have the narcissism of Iron Man or the God-like status of Thor. Spider-Man has vulnerabilities and, like Superman, he's wholesome and very much the family-friendly superhero.

Created in comic book form in the 1960s, I was aware of the 1970s Spider-Man TV show, with its funky soundtrack and imaginative special effects. Yet in 2002, a brand-new *Spider-Man* film leapt onto the big screen with Tobey Maguire in the role, with top-notch CGI and more emphasis on the teenage life of Peter Parker.

Behind the heroic mask of Spider-Man, Peter Parker's parents are dead and he's raised by his Aunt May and

Uncle Ben. While Peter battles the feelings in his heart over Mary Jane (Kirsten Dunst) and, ultimately, the Green Goblin, Uncle Ben acts as Peter's moral compass and utters the immortal line, "With great power comes great responsibility."

Cliff Robertson adds integrity and vulnerability to the role of Uncle Ben, while Tobey Maguire is a great Spider-Man and an even better Peter Parker. Outside his Spider-Man suit, Peter's a regular teenager with everyday real-world issues – he's bullied at school and has a crush on Mary Jane, his next-door neighbour. So, he's not a million miles away from your typical teenager. Yet, during a talk with young people, Spider-Man didn't top the poll as the most popular superhero.

Neither did the *X Men* franchise. Even with a steady stream of mutants gaining their strength and overcoming every bad guy due to their diversity, the long-running franchise prompted little discussion.

The wholesome but seemingly invincible Superman also stirred minimal discussion as Batman, the caped crusader, topped the poll as the go-to superhero in conversation with young people.

After a run of Bat-flicks beginning in 1989 and throughout the 1990s, in 2005, *Batman Begins* flew onto the screen with a fresh approach and an attempt to offer a different, more "grown-up" take on the caped crusader. Many young people would have been in the nursery when *Batman Begins* was doing the rounds at the cinema, yet they regularly pointed to this Bat-entry as the film that reinvigorated the character, allowing for a much more character-driven superhero film.

Directed by Christopher Nolan, *Batman Begins* jettisons the more campish aspects of his last cinema outing (*Batman and Robin* from 1997) and plays this Batman much straighter, as Batman's gadgets and Batmobile are either rejected or redesigned military equipment in a more plausible world of criminal gangs.

Batman Begins is more about Bruce Wayne (played by Christian Bale) than Batman, his trauma and the goals he puts in front of himself. He has a tragic past and an internal struggle; he's fallible and human. Yet, when Bruce sticks on his bat suit and gets behind the wheel of his Batmobile, he's a superhero – a hero who seemingly connects to young people.

"See the love shine in through my cracks. See the light shine out through me?"

During Pride Month, a group discussed films with LGBTQ+ storylines. As someone who had grown up with Les Dawson and Benny Hill blaring away each evening on the television, this was a chance to learn more about how young people view the world, as they're the ones with the fresh eyes.

The conversation began with the landmark Western drama *Brokeback Mountain*, which depicts a love story between two male cowboys. After a quick look on Google, the conversation moved on to a movie I was more familiar with, the 1961 British film *Victim*, starring Dirk Bogarde as barrister Melville Farr – a film which helped change the law on homosexuality in the UK.

The film that seemed to get the most airtime was called

Pariah – a gritty drama about Alike (Adepero Oduye), a seventeen-year-old black woman who gradually embraces her identity as a lesbian. Alike lives with her younger sister Sharonda (Sahra Mellesse), her bible-thumping mother Audrey (Kim Wayans), who can't or refuses to see who her daughter truly is, and Arthur (Charles Parnell), Alike's weathered and affectionate police officer father.

Living with her family, Alike chooses her own path in life, with the narrative hitting all the right notes as we follow her struggle to keep her sexuality a secret from her parents.

Aided by a beautiful and sincere central performance by Adepero Oduye, *Pariah* is a compelling film, undoubtedly better suited for a more mature young person. More a coming-out film than a coming-of-age film, *Pariah* reveals the teenage struggle of being someone your parents hope you are and who you *really* are deep down inside.

Beautifully shot and performed by a stellar cast, *Pariah* speaks to many about the difficulty of finding that first love, as Alike must navigate the feelings of her own heart. The story and its central themes of acceptance, identity and freedom offer the LGBTQ+ community a voice and a story that will resonate with many young people.

"How James Bond Saved My Life"

It's a fantastic feeling when young people share their favourite films with me, movies that entertain, inspire, speak to them or encourage them at such a difficult age. The film titles suggested to me by young people, like *Black*

Panther, *The Maze Runner* or *Batman Begins*, help shine a light on their personalities; it helped me better understand their world.

Young people are impressionable, and the power of screen heroes can be a shield from reality. As a young person bullied at school, cinematic role models transported me from a dark place to a bright new world filled with possibilities. I found a different thought pattern and a break from reality.

All these films, from *Stage Fright* to *Pariah*, can empower, challenge and entertain a young person or anyone who needs that moment to switch off and immerse themselves in another world, character or thought-provoking situation.

As for the films where I found a cinematic role model, there's still that warm glow of recognition seeing Groucho and Harpo; I still laugh at their films as I remember my past laughter as a child. Others, like Bond or Indiana Jones, were role models from another world, a welcome intrusion into mainstream life.

The cinematic heroes we love connect to us and become a part of us. As a child, watching cinematic role models was a successful method of cinema therapy, which helped me through periods at school when the bullying became too much, especially when I couldn't speak properly.

Bond films, in particular, assured me of a world where good would always triumph over evil – a promise of certainty in an uncertain world. Watching these onscreen heroes, I found freedom and distraction. I found my voice.